Field Guide to the Mountain Dulcimer
Book 1

By Anne Dodson

To access the online audio go to:

WWW.MELBAY.COM/30608MEB

Audio Contents
Book 1

Titles in italics are exercises, others are tunes or songs.
For details on downloading and using the audio files, see page 7.

Table of Contents
Book 1

Dedication

The summer before he died, my dad said to me, "Annie, I'm afraid that I gave you and David the idea that you had to be some kind of artists." I said, "If you did, then thank you very much."

This book is dedicated to my wondrous and supportive father, mother and brother:

Ted, Phyl and David Dodson

To all the Healds and Haags

And to my extended family:

Don and Pat Szostak
Christine, Dennis, Gabriel, Chloe and Marielle Faucher
John Szostak, Hiroko Sakurai and Kai Szostak
Liz, Charles, Noémie, Mia and Lily Clerc
Mary Kate Small

And to my loving husband, Matt ("he who notices things") Szostak, who brings light and laughter to my life, and without whom this book would still be silently waiting in pieces in the cowboy room.

Acknowledgements and Credits

What would I do without...

So many people have helped with this book, over many years. Thank you to all my dulcimer students/friends who have helped me clarify how I communicate and let me experiment on them, all with unwavering humor and diplomacy.

Thank you, Asha Stager, for your friendship, insights, musical contributions and for sharing your many skills. You keep me on my toes – literally!

Thanks to Kat Logan for your wonderful and playful artwork as well as your guiding spirit.

Thanks to Cindy Kallet, Grey Larsen, Loie Lyman, Will Brown, John Renbourn, Cathryn Ward, Steve Sellors, Gordon Bok and Carol Rohl – supportive friends all.

Thank you to John Blodgett and Ken Gross for technical advice, and to Bob and Janita Baker of *Blue Lion Instruments* for my lovely dulcimers.

Thanks to Bill Bay and the crew at Mel Bay for guidance through the world of book publishing.

This book would never have come to fruition without Matt, Cindy and Grey. You kept me from talking myself into too many holes. Thank you guys!

Credits

All illustrations and photographs by Kat Logan, except childhood photo by Phyllis Dodson
Audio files recorded by Anne Dodson and processed by Anne Dodson and Matt Szostak
Layout and editing by Anne Dodson and Matt Szostak
Additional notation editing by Grey Larsen
Proofreading by Matt Szostak, Grey Larsen, Cindy Kallet and Asha Stager
Computer expertise and infinite patience by Matt Szostak

Introduction to Book 1
I know – I never read introductions either. But read this one.

Welcome to Book 1 of "Field Guide to the Mountain Dulcimer," the first in a series of two books. This volume contains Level I, and you'll find Levels II and III in Book 2.

A little background

A number of years ago I taught a gifted young dulcimer student. Because of her age and her obvious talent, I decided that each week I would write a piece of music that would help her to understand a new skill. Occasionally I would throw in an arrangement of a well-known folk song or carol, but most of the pieces were original. She wrote a few herself.

My young student grew up, her interests changed and she stopped taking lessons, but I'd gotten into the habit of writing these tunes. I found they worked equally well in workshops and in lessons with adults. As this material began to take shape, I realized that I'd need to write exercises to demonstrate what I usually show by example. Through years of experimenting, I discovered the mix of exercises and original and familiar tunes and songs that seemed most helpful to students, and that is what I share here with you.

Eventually, it became obvious that I was actually writing two books. Book 1 (Level I) is a beginner's guide containing information on how to buy, maintain and start playing mountain dulcimer, and Book 2 (Levels II and III) continues on with more advanced techniques.

How this book works

This book is laid out in the same manner as I would teach a private student, from simple one-line tunes up through more complicated arrangements.

Here's how "Field Guide to the Mountain Dulcimer, Book 1" is organized:
- It begins with an overview of the material that we'll be covering.
- Each chapter begins with an explanation of its goals, and then moves on to exercises and tunes that support the new skills and concepts being presented.
- It closes off with a chapter called "Take a Break," in which you get to play tunes designed to reinforce the skills you've been working on.
- And finally, there's an introduction to Book 2 to let you know what you've got waiting for you!

With my private students, I try to teach by ear, eye and example and only use the written music as back up – something to take home to help remember the lesson. Since we can't do that here, we have to rely on "tablature," or "TAB" for short.

So what's that? TAB is kind of a guided tour of the fretboard that shows your left hand exactly where it needs to go. We'll get into it in depth in the chapter called "Basics." Although it's necessary to use tablature to communicate ideas within the limitations of a book, I hope you'll use it as a guide – not a crutch. I encourage you to make your playing a reflection of your own artistic expression.

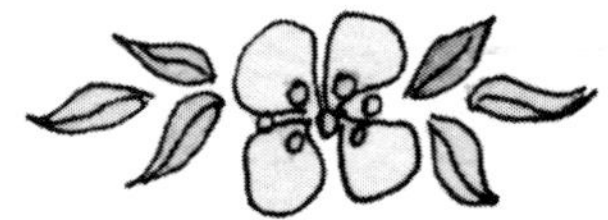

The companion downloadable audio files

You can download accompanying online audio files that let you hear the exercises and the tunes. This is important, as many of the pieces will be new to you. I suggest that you:

- **Read the text.**
- Listen to the music.
- Reread the text.
- Play the exercise(s) or tune.
- Repeat the above in any order until it all becomes clear.

I'm one of those people who, when I bring home a new camera, starts poking at the buttons and can't understand why it doesn't work. My husband says, "What does the manual say?"… and I say, "Manual?" The exercises and tunes are designed to give you less talk and more "example," but imagine coming to me for a lesson and having me never explain anything to you. You need to read the text as *well* as listen and play. You do that, and next time I'll read the camera manual. Deal?

 When you see this icon, you'll know there is a recorded music file available. The track number leads you to the correct exercise, song or tune. You'll find a complete list of the audio contents on page 2.

To download these files, go to www.melbay.com/30608MEB

You will not find recorded sound files for chord charts – only for exercises, songs and tunes. Note that for tunes written with repeated parts that sound the same, I didn't play the repeats in the audio files.

So what kind of dulcimer do you have, and what does that mean?
Three strings, four strings and the double first string

With the dulcimer on your lap, the string closest to you, the highest pitched, is called the first string. The traditional mountain dulcimer style is to play melody only on the first string (or first two if they are close together), leaving the remaining strings open as drones. It's a wonderful sound, and you'll be playing in this manner for the first few exercises in this book. When playing traditionally, people often use a noter – basically a small stick – in their left hand to play those first-string notes. You can make a simple noter by cutting a four-inch piece of pencil-size doweling, or you can buy (or make) a fancier one. I use a noter so infrequently that I won't discuss them further, but there are many books on traditional playing where you can find more information.

Take a look at the following three illustrations in which the bottom line represents the first string:

"Three-string dulcimer" refers to a dulcimer that has three strings spaced like this…

…or has four strings in the traditional setup of a double first string:

That's still considered a three-string instrument. The double first setup, with the two strings close together, is designed to give more volume to the melody so that it rises above the drones when playing in the traditional style. If you have a three-string dulcimer with a double first (four strings total), I recommend that you remove one of the double pair. Once you start playing chords, or playing melodies on all your strings (which you'll be doing soon), it's much easier to use a single first string.

"Four-string dulcimer" refers to instruments with four equidistant strings – four strings evenly spaced across the fretboard like this…

If your instrument is set up in such a way that there's the possibility of using four equidistant strings, I strongly recommend that arrangement.[1] It gives a balance to your right hand (three strings always feels like limping to me when I'm finger-picking) and it lets the second string operate as an additional drone. It can create some wonderful and unexpected chords. You quickly become adept at adapting three-string tablature to four strings.

Three- and four-string dulcimers are the most common, but occasionally you may find dulcimers that have five, six, seven, eight or more strings. These are usually designed to accommodate double strings on any or all strings.

Most of the tunes in this book, however, are arranged for three-string dulcimer, as that's what most people play. Added material pertaining only to those of you who are playing four-string equidistant instruments is written in *italics*. If you're playing a three-string dulcimer, you can skip right over sections written in italics. *If you have four equidistant strings (like me), at first you'll use your second string as a drone when you're strumming, and you'll ignore the poor thing when you're fingerpicking. In Book 2, Level III, your second string will find its own identity! If you're playing with four equidistant strings, you can play any of the three-string arrangements.*

Because I play with four equidistant strings, sometimes you'll hear my open drone string ringing through in the audio files, especially when I'm strumming. If you're playing with a three-string setup, don't let that confuse you.

My theory about theory…

Unless you have a background in music, theory can feel like a murky, dark swamp. In sections that discuss music theory, you may not follow everything on a first read-through. But it's worth plowing through, letting your understanding build as you go along. Be patient with yourself.

…and what is all this about a 6½ fret?

Put your dulcimer on your lap. Look at the fretboard. You'll notice there are big spaces and little spaces between the frets (those metal bars). If you look at a guitar you'll see consistent spacing between frets, getting gradually smaller as you progress up the fretboard. So what's the difference, you ask? Well, the guitar is a chromatic instrument. Think of the white AND the black keys on a piano. Now look at your dulcimer again and think of only the white keys (basically… more about this later). That's called diatonic. So you're missing some notes, and if you put frets in the middle of the big spaces then you'd have those notes – and you'd have a chromatic dulcimer. But being diatonic is one of the things that I find distinctive about the instrument.

But, there is one concession that dulcimer builders have made over the years, and your dulcimer may or may not have it – that being a "6½" fret. Here's how you know if you have it. When you strum across the fretboard, you call that "zero" or "open." If you press down just to the left of the 1st fret on the string closest to you, that's fret #1 and so on up the fretboard. When you get to #5, look to the right. Are there three small frets close together or is there a short space and then another long one? If you have the three close together then your

---

[1] More about this later in the chapter – see "buying a dulcimer."

dulcimer has a 6½ fret. That's non-traditional, but very, very good to have in my opinion. No 6½ fret? Too bad; if you like your dulcimer and aren't thinking of upgrading it, then there are playing techniques that you can use to work around the absence of the 6½ fret. Another option is to have a new fret put in your present instrument. This book will be difficult to use if you don't have it.

People ask me why we label it 6½ rather than just call it 7. Well, say you live at #6 Mockingbird Lane and your next-door neighbor is at #7 Mockingbird Lane and then somebody builds a house in the empty lot between you. The post office is going to give your new neighbors an address of 6½ Mockingbird Lane because otherwise, most of the street is going to have to change their address. Got it?

Here's what the two different layouts look like – the horizontal lines represent the strings of a three-string dulcimer *(fret spacing is the same for four-string setup)*; the numbered vertical lines represent the frets:

Traditional fretboard layout – no 6½ fret:

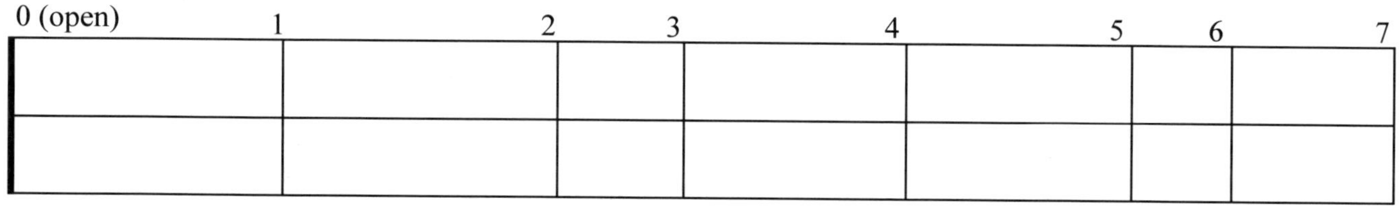

0 (open)   1   2 3   4   5 6   7

Fretboard layout with 6½ fret:

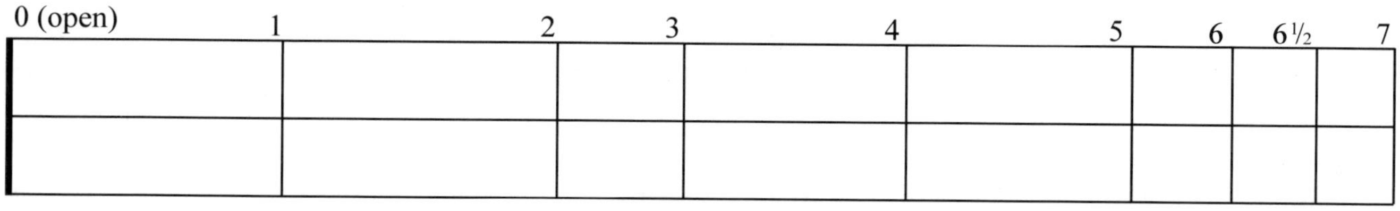

0 (open)   1   2 3   4   5 6 6½ 7

A new trend is to add a 1½ fret. Some like it, some don't. I don't have it on any of my instruments, but I understand why it could be fun and useful. Just know it could be there and is yet another option.

Tuning and electronic tuners

Dulcimer tunings are explained as you need them in later chapters. In terms of actually tuning the instrument, there is debate about electronic tuners; are they a crutch that keeps you from learning to tune by ear or are they an aid that helps you learn to tune? The bottom line is that tuning can be extremely frustrating, to the point where I've seen people give up. So, although they can be a crutch, I'm quite in favor of electronic tuners. Look for a phone app, or you can get a small, inexpensive chromatic tuner at any music store. Ask them to show you how to use it. Once you get the idea, try tuning by ear and then see how you did by checking with the tuner. It takes time to learn to tune by ear, but it's a skill worth developing. Make sure you're buying a chromatic tuner and not a guitar tuner, which only registers the open notes on a guitar.

Getting your instrument in tune

All of the tunes in Book 1 are in a traditional tuning called Mixolydian. If you have three strings, you tune them to DAD (1-5-8).[2] Your bass string, or third string, gets tuned to a D note. It's the biggest string, farthest away from you and is also lowest in pitch. Your middle string, or second string, is the A. Then you tune the first string, which is the string closest to you, to a D note, which is an octave above your bass string. Four-string dulcimers, equidistant setup or not, tune to DADD (1-5-8-8) with the first two strings in unison.

This is the tuning you want to start with. You can tune the instrument to itself by doing the following:
- Tune the bass string to a D note.
- Then press down just to the left of the 4th fret on your bass string. That will be an A and you tune your middle string to that pitch.
- Tune the high D string(*s*) to the pitch created by pressing down just to the left of the 3rd fret on your A string.

If that all feels like too much, then I suggest that for now you get those notes from a fixed-pitch instrument, like a piano or an electronic tuner.

Included in Book 2 are tunes in DGD/DGDD (1-4-8/1-4-8-8), DAC/DADC (1-5-7/1-5-8-7) and some that utilize a capo. There is one common dulcimer tuning that I've never spent much time with, which is DAA (1-5-5). It's a lovely tuning, but I use it rarely. Although it is not included in either Book 1 or Book 2, many of the concepts that you'll be learning will be transferable to any tuning.

Styles of playing, mutiny in Michigan and an explanation of what's different about this book

One of the challenges of playing dulcimer is that there is very little standardization. There are standard tunings, but what is done with them varies from player to player. There are a few well-known builders, but most of the instruments students bring to me are home-built or made by people I've never heard of. There are regional differences as well. While students in workshops in New England are usually happy when I teach in DAD, I thought I was going to end up with a mutiny on my hands at a workshop in Michigan. They all played in DAA and did *not* want to change. It made for an interesting few hours.[3]

So what are you supposed to do with all these choices? Start with what you've got and don't think you have to learn it all or at least not all at once. If you don't own an instrument, see the section on "buying a dulcimer." This book is designed to be a step-by-step method for learning to play, but remember that it's the way that *I* play – not the full spectrum of what is possible on the dulcimer.

If you see chord names (i.e. "D," "G") written over the music, they are generally put there for a second, accompanying part… say, for another dulcimer, or a guitarist or to accompany singing. They are usually the chords you're playing as defined by the tablature, except in a few cases.

This book is unique in that it contains many original pieces. Wouldn't it be easier to learn with music you know already? There are roughly 1,243,758 dulcimer songbooks with arrangements for tunes that you know. Although unfamiliar tunes may offer a bit more of a challenge, many of the tunes (and most of the exercises) have been written specifically to help you learn a particular technique.

---

[2] If the number system (i.e. 1-5-8) doesn't make sense to you, don't worry about it for now; we'll go into it in depth later, in Book 2. You'll notice that I use 1-5-8 (or 1-5-8-8) instead of 8-5-1 (8-8-5-1). In the dulcimer world you're going to see it written both ways.

[3] I have recovered, but thanks for asking.

Buying a dulcimer

If you don't actually have an instrument yet, what you've been reading should give you some idea of your options. Here are a few more thoughts about buying your first dulcimer.

Probably the biggest help I can give you is this: when you go to the music store, take someone with you who already plays and whose playing you admire. I strongly recommend getting an instrument with a 6½ fret, and geared tuning pegs as opposed to friction pegs. It should also have the capability of being able to change from four strings, with the first two being close together (traditional style), to four equidistant strings. Being able to accommodate those two different setups is as easy as adding two extra grooves to the nut and saddle – the grooved supports at the head and tail of the instrument that the strings pass over. If you buy an instrument with only three strings, with no possibility of adding a fourth or of changing the setup to four equidistant strings, you limit what you'll be able to do in the future. Most instruments can have a new nut and saddle added, but unless you absolutely fall in love with an instrument that is "nut and saddle challenged," why not choose an instrument with the most options?

Even if you can't play the dulcimer yet, put the instrument that you're considering buying on your lap and press down on the strings. Are they hard to press down? Does it feel good to you? Have your dulcimer-playing friend play it. Don't ever let anyone pressure you into buying an instrument.

Although there are many excellent regional builders, there are also some acknowledged, recognized names out there. If you thumb through a music magazine (especially something like "Dulcimer Players News"[4]), you'll find listings of festivals, information about builders and players, and even the occasional advertisement for a dulcimer cruise!

I play two different *Blue Lion* mountain dulcimers. One is their standard professional model and the other is a bass (a full octave lower). Most of the time I have them set up with four equidistant strings rather than a double first. Both the sound and the way they are built seem to suit my hands and my ears. One of my instruments has fancy inlays; the other is more basic. The aesthetic extras don't make a difference in the sound but the kind of wood that is used does. Certain woods will make the instrument sound richer and fuller. I invested in high-end woods for both of my instruments, but if you're not planning on playing professionally, that may not be a priority for you.

If you order an instrument – from *any* builder – you have the advantage of getting exactly what you want. On the other hand, you don't get to play it until it's yours. If it's truly not your instrument, some builders will let you return it, but that's a tough call. It *is* how they make their living. But before you order an instrument, make sure that you know the builder's policies and how long it will take for your dulcimer to be delivered to you.

Basically, rely on your instincts but hedge your bets with as much help as you can get from friends or professionals you might hire to help you. I've seen some absolutely gorgeous instruments that sounded terrible or were difficult to play. It helps if the builder is also a player. You want to find a builder who makes playability a priority.

Left-handed players

There are two theories concerning left-handed players learning to play the dulcimer – both compelling. I have left-handers in my family and I've watched them struggle with people's expectations for them to convert to

---

[4] **DPN** is a magazine dedicated to both mountain dulcimers and hammered dulcimers.

using their right hands for many things – not just instrument playing. With that in mind, my initial reaction is to have you switch the strings around and play left-handed.

However, my most recent way of looking at it comes from my friend, John Blodgett, an instrument builder whom I greatly admire. He suggests starting out right-handed and seeing how it goes. Since stringed instruments take two hands to play, with both hands doing intelligent work, as a left-handed player you may be strong with chords and melodic work, and not as strong with strumming and fingerpicking. That may not be a bad trade-off.

There are other advantages to trying to play right-handed. Your choice of instruments will be greater, and when you go dulcimer shopping you'll be able to try them out. If you go to a party without your dulcimer, you'll be able to play other people's instruments. On the other hand, I had it pointed out to me by a left-handed player that he thought one of the advantages of a left-handed setup was that if you go to a party, other people *won't* be able to play your instrument, so there you go.

When I take on a new student who is left-handed, I start them out with a right-handed setup. Most people have felt it's worked fine for them. One or two have felt that they were swimming upstream and we've changed the strings around so they were more comfortable. It's an individual decision. I apologize that this book is right-hand oriented and hope that you can make the changes as you need to if you're playing left-handed.

The drawings

The playful illustrations in this book were created by Maine artist and musician, Kat Logan. You'll see two in particular pop up quite often, indicating the following:

"In a nutshell" is a synopsis of a concept or chapter.

The teacup means that you might want to take some time to work on an exercise or tune. I once had a student who complained that she could play fine at home but when she got to her lesson she became self-conscious. One day I made tea while she played; she did fine. From then on I made tea when she first arrived and I pretended to not listen!

Some final thoughts

1) If you find yourself lost in instructions, or if something doesn't make sense to you, try reading the passage again *out loud*. Sections that include a series of directions
   - are
   - written
   - with
   - bullets

2) Most of the tunes in this book were named for actual events. Some deserve an explanation – most don't. You could say that this book is a non-chronological autobiography!

3) When I refer to "Asha," I'm talking about my friend Asha Stager, who wrote or co-wrote some of the tunes you'll encounter. She, along with a long list of other "proofers," have dedicated many hours to making me look good, or at least better than I would have if some mistakes and basic confusions hadn't been cleared up by their diligent work.[5]

4) Take a lesson from a 7-year old student of mine who, when asked if she'd practiced said, "well… no… but I played a lot."

So plow in. And have fun playing!

Anne Dodson

---

[5] Most common quote from the ever-polite proofers: *"Ah, Anne… is this bit a… typo?"*

Care and Feeding of Your Dulcimer
Co-authored by John Blodgett

John Blodgett is an instrument builder who works at Woodsound Studio in Rockport, Maine. He is also the man I entrust with the care of my instruments. This chapter is a combination of our thoughts and words.

The shocking facts

The main words here are heat, cold, humidity and shock (extremes in temperature, dropping and crushing).

Heat is a big one; most instruments are put together with heat-soluble glue. Enough said? Well, perhaps not; melting glue = instrument comes apart in many pieces = one very bad day. In the summer or in hot climates keep your instrument away from direct heat sources and don't leave it in a car any more than you would a pet. In the winter be aware of heat vents, heaters, stoves, etc., when putting your dulcimer down.

Most instruments can tolerate cold better than heat, but you want to avoid extremes and sudden temperature changes in general. If it's been inside a cold car, for instance, bring it inside, but keep it wrapped, preferably in a case. Leave it sealed for longer than you think you need to. Then you might crack the case a tiny bit, but if you notice it sweating, close it right back up. Open the case by increments. How long the process takes depends on how cold it was to begin with. You should be fine, say, going a short distance to a party in a heated car. Just be cautious and aware.

Temperature extremes can not only cause structural nightmares; they can also adversely affect the finish. Ask to look at my classical guitar sometime. One winter it was late for a live radio broadcast (silly guitar), after traveling in a cold car. We were on the air *now*. I watched and *listened* in wonderment as the finish on the top face spread out magnificently into uncountable small lines. I know of which I speak.

Humidity

Another issue is humidity. This is especially important with a newly built instrument. New instruments have a breaking-in period during which they are more susceptible to environmental conditions. I live on the coast of Maine, which is damp in the summer and very dry, because of heating systems, in the winter. Summer is fine, but in the winter there is the risk of the wood cracking from getting too dry. Wood is alive. It expands across the grain (width but not length) when it gains humidity, and contracts when dry, just like a hardwood floor.

There are methods to keep your dulcimer from drying out. I've seen little rubber hoses stamped with holes, with a sponge inside, that actually go inside a sound hole. I've seen little plastic boxes, with absorbent material inside, that go into the case. They all seem to work, although you need to think "damp," not "wet," when you're using these devices. We humidify our house and not each individual instrument.

If your dulcimer was built in a dry climate then you might not need to humidify it during the winter, but that's unusual. I've even met an instrument or two that needed to be *de*-humidified in the summer months (although that's such a novel idea to me that I could hardly type that last sentence). Ask the builder or salesperson what he/she recommends for humidity; most instruments are built at 40-50% relative humidity and are happiest in that range.

Dropping and crushing

Try not to.

Action and strings

I find that most of my instruments make a shift in the fall as they dry out and then again in the spring when they gain back some humidity. This can affect the action, which is a term that defines how high the strings are off the fingerboard. If the action is too high, your instrument can be harder to play than it needs to be. If it's too low, you can get buzzes. Fret buzz can also be a result of bumps in the fingerboard or a loose fret, both of which can usually be fixed easily by a professional. But it's not quite as cut-and-dried as that.

How you set the action depends upon how you play the instrument and the gauge of the strings that you use. If you primarily use a flat pick and you play hard, then you want to go for heavier strings and higher action. On dulcimers, the standard height for action is $^1/_{16}$ inch – $^1/_8$ inch, measured from the top of the fret to the underside of the string at the octave (7th) fret.

If, like me, you tend to fingerpick and generally play gently, then you want to use lighter strings and lower action. I've never liked the gauges of the sets that come prepackaged for dulcimers, and they tend to contain a nickel wound string, which I don't like. For the lowest string I use a .024w brass or bronze wound string.[1] For the middle string I use a .014, and for my first string(*s*) I use .011. You need to check and see if the strings on your instrument are attached with a loop end or a ball end and make sure you get the appropriate one.

If you're a *very* delicate player, or like to play fast tunes with lots of left hand work, you might like to try even lighter gauge strings. However, if you have a heavy right hand, then very light strings could cause problems. You just have to experiment, depending upon how you like to play, and come up with string gauges and action that suit you and your instrument.

You don't have to go far to change the gauge. Here are some appropriate range ideas:
- If the .011 feels too heavy, try .010. Too light? Try .012.
- For the .014, you could lighten up to .013 or make it heavier with a .015.
- If your bass string, the .024w, needs to go lighter, try .022w. Fatten it up with .026w.

How often you change strings depends upon what you do with the instrument. If you're performing or recording you might change them more often than someone who is playing simply for their own enjoyment. In an ideal world, if you wash your hands before playing and wipe your strings down at the end of a playing session, your strings will last longer. I rarely remember.

If your strings are rusty or corroded, that's an obvious message that it's time to change them. However, there are more subtle clues that your strings are getting old. Is it hard to tune or does it play out of tune, even when you use an electronic tuner? Is the response of the strings, especially when you're playing hammer-ons and pull-offs, a little sluggish?

Over time strings actually lose their stretch. They begin to feel stiffer than when you first put them on because they are! When they lose their elasticity they sound sharp, so it becomes impossible to play in tune.

---

[1] The number used to identify the size of a string is actually its diameter, in inches.

When I was performing full time, I changed my strings every week or two. I'm performing less these days and I might go months before changing them. I'll often change them a day or two in advance of recording or performing.

Sometimes in the spring or fall, the changes in my instruments are big enough that I need to have the action adjusted. Most years I notice the difference but it's within my tolerance. Many players know how to adjust the action themselves.

And, speaking of doing things for yourself, if you've never changed strings on an instrument, ask the builder or salesperson for instruction – with a demonstration if possible – when you buy your dulcimer.

Setup and intonation

With a new student, the first thing I do is play their dulcimer. Even an instrument that looks gorgeous can be a nightmare to play, either because it has problems with its basic structure or because it's not set up properly.

If you're having problems with playing that don't go away with practice, take it to someone who knows what they're doing and make sure there isn't either some basic organic problem with the instrument or something wrong with the way it's set up.

It's extremely important that the intonation is correct on your instrument. Intonation has to do with where the nut and the saddle (the grooved supports that hold the strings above the fingerboard) are placed in relationship to the octave (7th) fret.[2] If the intonation is off, you can tune your open strings perfectly and still have the instrument out of tune with itself when you start fretting. Be suspicious if things sound fine when you're playing close to the headstock but sound questionable as you move up the fretboard, or if your instrument seems impossible to tune.

Proper setup can make a world of difference in how you enjoy the experience of playing. Furthermore, you can't sing in tune with an instrument that is out of tune. Whether you're accompanying yourself or playing instrumentals, you can ruin your ear training and sense of pitch by regularly playing an instrument that is not in tune with itself. Having the intonation adjusted is no big deal, but is vital to your dulcimer's playability and to your growth as a musician.

Final thoughts

Here are a few – perhaps obvious, but perhaps not – final thoughts, taken from personal experience:
- Instruments are kid magnets.
- Don't leave your dulcimer lying on the floor or a stage.
- It's okay to say no to someone who wants to play your instrument.
- If you're performing, make sure that the microphones are firmly placed in their clips.
- Gravity usually wins.
- Instrument lust is real. One is never enough. Succumb whenever possible.
- And, no matter how frustrated you get when you're practicing, the wood stove is not a viable answer (no personal experience thus far).

---

[2] F.Y.I., the octave is half the vibrating string length.

Blank TAB sheets
Capturing your own most excellent inspiration!

The following two pages are blank sheets for tablature – one for three strings, one for four strings. Make a few copies, and if you find yourself writing, notate it. *If you're playing four-string equidistant you may find that the three-string TAB will be enough at this stage. I tend to notate using three-string TAB – that's what you'll be working with for this book anyway!*

If you've never written music before, here are a few suggestions that might help you:
- Document what you compose. You'll think at the time of inspiration that you'll remember it. If you're like me, you won't – it's a lot like a dream in that way.
- It doesn't have to be a complete piece – a measure or a line might expand into something more later on.
- Record what's "arriving." A little, cheap recorder will do – it doesn't have to be fancy. You may already have one on your phone!
- Notate, as well, on blank TAB. Write the notes into the music staff if you are able. If not, just write in the tablature lines, but do try to indicate the rhythm.
- Most of us censor our own creative process. Get those ideas down without thinking that you have to create an "important piece" (although you might!). You're getting an idea down so you don't lose it.

I often encourage students to write, and they are always surprised and delighted by what comes out, as am I. There can be a subtle, yet exciting shift when you change the process from that of interpreting another musician's ideas to taking control of your own creativity.

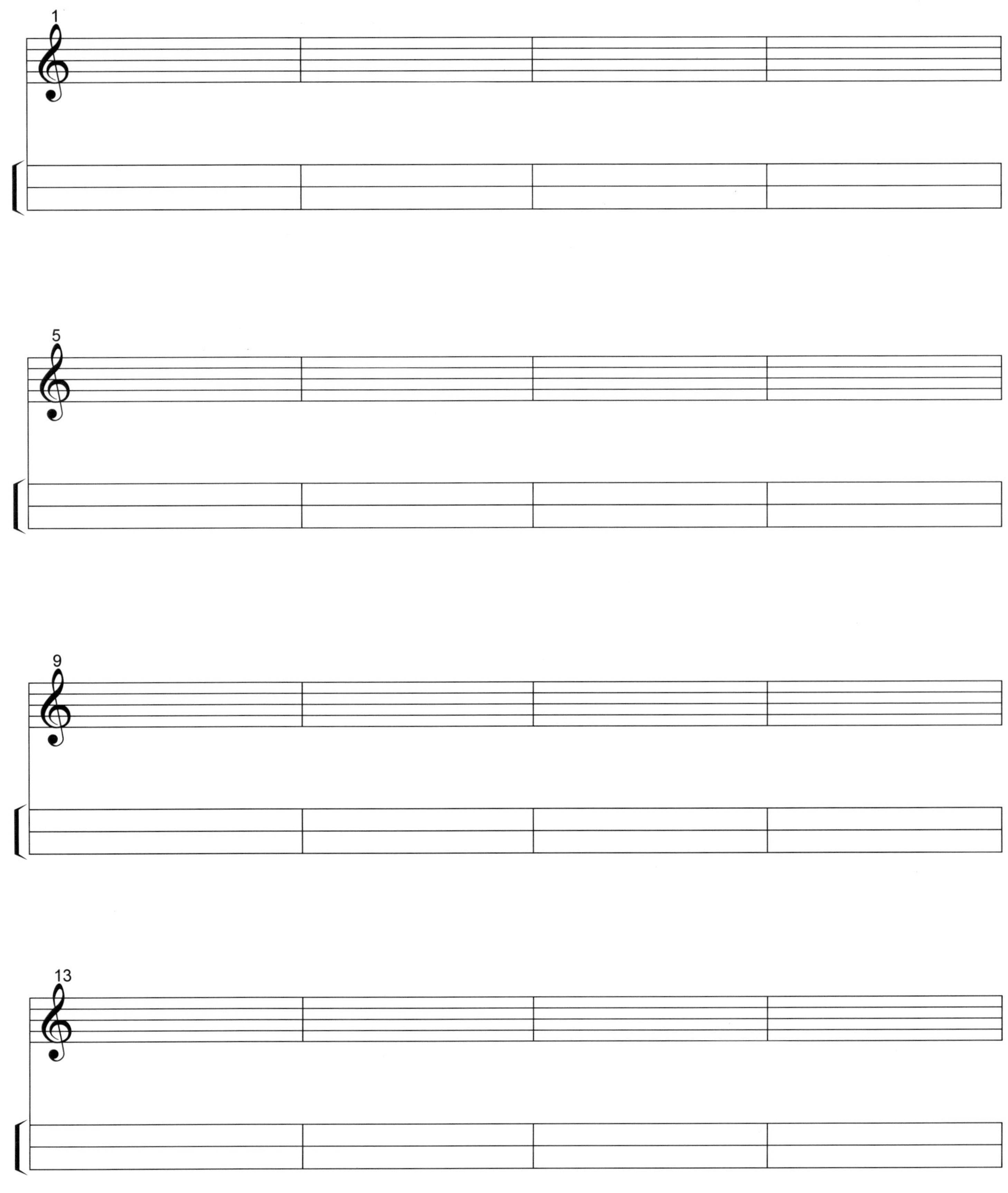

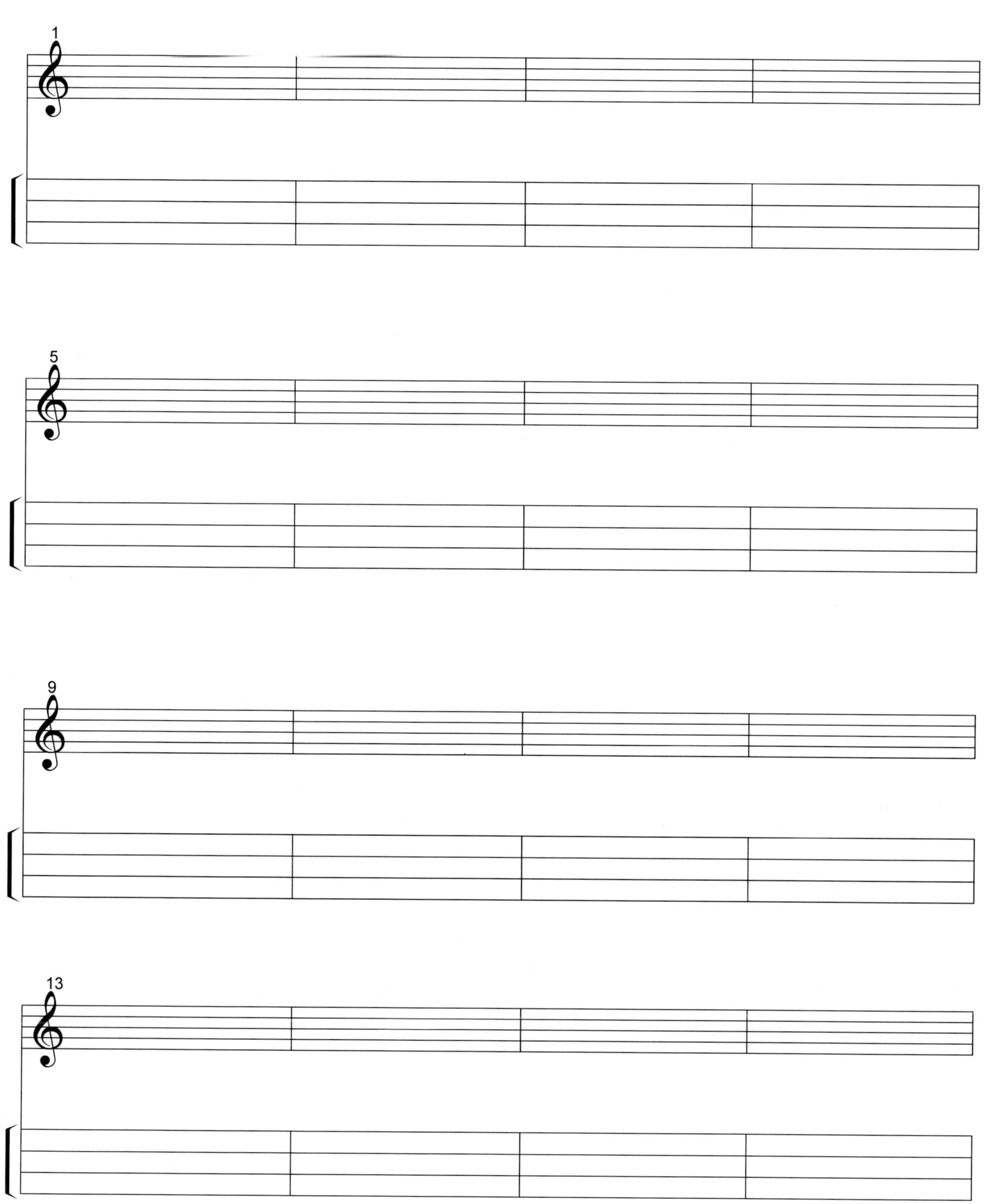

Level I
The Basics

Introduction to Level I

 Book 1, Level I is a beginner's guide, addressing buying, tuning, holding and care of the instrument, as well as learning to play simple melodies, and chords in different positions. You'll also find basic right and left hand techniques and, at the end, some tunes to play that reinforce what you've learned throughout the book.

That's it in a nutshell! But here are a few hints for making the process easy and fun:

If you're learning to juggle, you start with one ball, throwing it from hand to hand. Then you add a second ball until you get comfortable. Only then do you go to a third, and if you start dropping balls, you go back to two.[1] It's the same with the dulcimer – when you start something new and you run into trouble, think about what you can eliminate. Can you simplify the right hand if you're concentrating on a new left hand technique? If you're trying something new with the right hand, can you only do the right hand for a while?

As you work on these pieces, start by being strict with yourself about timing and consistent fingering. Once you get more control, feel free to play around. Experiment with speeding up a section, slow down another. Find the passages that want to be louder or softer. Add extra notes – leave out notes. Often the expression lies in the spaces between the notes you play.

We all have old tapes running in our minds that make us feel bad about ourselves and our skills. Put that stuff aside and just enjoy yourself. Laugh when your brain and your hands are not in agreement; you'll get there. If you've taken on something challenging and are feeling overwhelmed, reward yourself by playing a piece you know well and love to play.

Think of problem areas as red flags that are telling you to do some concentrated work on that section. Work on that single phrase or measure. Isolate it to as tiny a section as you can. Play it slowly. Get it down. Remember to use consistent fingering. Now expand it – add the measure before or after. Get that down. Then and only then do you put it back into the whole piece. If you don't take the time to work on problem areas, you'll always stumble at that point.

Recognize when something is just too much. There's a fine line between saying, "I can't do that," and, "I'm not ready for that," and it's different for each of us. Give it a good try. Really concentrate, but on a given day, if something isn't working, then simplify or go back to a piece that's easier for you. Try again later. Something you struggle with now you may find very simple when you come back to it in a day, a week, a month.

At this point I have to assume that you have a basic understanding of written music, such as the differences between meters (i.e. 3/4 and 4/4 timing), and the relative values of a whole note, half note, quarter note, etc. You should also understand that notes get higher in pitch as they move up the staff, and it would be helpful, though not essential, if you know the names of notes on the treble clef. A familiarity with the layout of a piano keyboard wouldn't hurt either.

If your answer is "hmmm," there are some wonderful books pertaining to the mechanics of written music as well as basic theory. But if you're on the fence, plow into the next chapter and see how you do.

Sometimes it helps to clap out the rhythm to a new piece before you add the notes or chords. Again, it's a matter of cutting down on the number of new things you're trying to do at the same time.

---

[1] (Confession: I've never been able to juggle.)

Some people get stuck in the rut of only playing what is familiar. Or, they will only play from tablature. Or, they challenge themselves so much that they get overwhelmed and give up. Your tolerance may shift from day to day. Treat each day separately and be kind to yourself. There are days for a challenge, days for using your music for comfort. But keep trying new things.

Take your time – move through the chapters at a pace that feels right to you, but go back and review or rework chapters. You're never going to get all the information in one reading. From my work with students, I know how often I have to repeat instructions. I once had a Russian teacher who, when I was frustrated with how long it took to get a new word in my head, said, "Anne – it takes an average of hearing a word *thirteen* times before you know it." I bet that's not an exaggeration!

When you're reading directions, it's remarkably easy to skim over a section. If you suspect that you're doing that, and missing something vital as a result, you might find it helpful to read instructions out loud. You may feel silly, but you may also save yourself some aggravation.

Two final things regarding the recordings I've made to accompany this book:
- Don't forget – since I play with four equidistant strings, you will occasionally hear my open D-string drone, especially during strums. If you're playing with a three-string setup, don't let that confuse you.
- I've made every attempt to interpret the TAB exactly as written, especially for exercises (successfully, I believe!). For tunes, you may encounter occasional minor differences between the written music and the recorded version.

Ready to start playing? Okay – first up… some basics.

Chapter 1 ~ The Basics

Holding the instrument

Sit in a chair that allows your thighs to be parallel with the floor. Place the instrument on your lap with the headstock to your left. Keep your knees apart to give the dulcimer a wider base on which to sit. The natural inclination is to keep the instrument close to your body (like the photo on the left), but if instead you move the headstock away from you a little bit, so that the right side of the instrument is closer to you than the left side, you'll have more room to navigate with your left hand and arm (like the photo on the right). Move the instrument away from you, out onto your knees as far as is comfortable. That will give you more room when you are playing up higher on the fretboard as well as let your arms hang in a relaxed position.

Not like this…

Like this!

Back-straps and such

You can buy or make a back-strap that helps to keep the instrument in place and lets your dulcimer sit farther away from your body than would otherwise be possible. That's what I use (see photos above). What you're trying to do is create space between your body and the dulcimer, allowing extra room for your hands and arms to navigate. If your instrument doesn't come with an end-pin (a metal or wooden button at the bottom end that holds one end of your back-strap), you may want to have one installed. You can also put one at the base of the headstock, although more often than not you can find a place to "tie on."

People have also come up with all kinds of inventions that involve knee-straps, boards and/or Velcro or non-slip rug mats to keep the dulcimer from slipping. Experiment and see what works best for you. None of these inventions are necessary but most people find them helpful. My students will attest to the fact that I frequently nag… er… suggest that they push their instrument farther out toward their knees.

Hand and body position

Shake your hands out and then let them fall naturally with the palm up. See how they form a relaxed arch? Now turn your hands over and you're in a good position to play. Most people start out trying to support their hand on the body of the instrument, with their left hand low (like the photo below on the left). Don't do that – keep your left hand slightly raised and parallel to the fretboard (like the photo on the right).

You want to keep the fingers of both hands rounded. With your left hand, try to keep the knuckles that are closest to the nail from flattening out ("caving in," "breaking"). You want the tips of your fingers to come straight down onto the string. The *only* way you can make that happen is by keeping your left-hand nails filed short enough that they don't interfere – anything longer than "almost-not-there" will cause your finger to flatten out. I keep my right nails a little longer for fingerpicking.

Not like this…

Like this!

As you begin to play, it's likely that your left shoulder will rise up and that your shoulders will tense up. You'll be concentrating and will forget to keep your body relaxed. Your brain can only take so many new challenges at once, so take frequent breaks to check your hand and body position, roll your shoulders and your neck, flex your hands. Keep your shoulders level and don't let your upper body follow the movements of your hands. Keep your elbows relaxed, close to your body but not "hugging" it.

Basic right hand fingering

There are several simple things that you can do with your right hand as you begin to get the feel of the instrument. In later chapters we'll deal with more advanced picking patterns and strums, but for now you need to develop a "survival" technique that will not distract from what you're learning with your left hand.

The most straightforward way to start with your right hand is simply to strum. This can be done with a flat pick or with your thumb or fingers. Many people starting out find that they are happiest with a big, on-the-soft-side flat pick. As you become more adept at flat-picking you will probably want to graduate to a smaller and harder pick.

Many beginners assume that they have to strum or pick far to the right, where the fretboard is cut out (left photo, below). I tend to let my right arm and hand fall naturally; for me that usually means strumming around the 9th fret (right photo, below). Experiment and see what you like. You might like one placement for one song, a different placement for another. Whether you're using fingers or a pick, start out by just strumming away from you. Get a feel for that. Then strum toward you. For now, that should be enough to get you going. We'll work more with the right hand in later chapters.

Different right hand positions

Basic left hand fingering

The tunes in Book 1 are all in what's called Mixolydian mode[1], in this case tuned to DAD or DADD (1-5-8 or 1-5-8-8). Whether it's DAD or DADD depends upon whether you're playing a dulcimer with three or four strings. DADD tuning applies to four equidistant strings (which is the way I generally play). It's also how you would tune a traditional double first string setup (see page 7).

With left hand fingering I don't use my pinkie as much as some players do. I do use my thumb a lot. People with long fingers often don't need to use their thumbs. Using only fingers can make for smoother and quicker left hand fingering – fingers generally move faster than a thumb – but using your thumb can really extend your reach. So if you have small hands, like me, then the thumb it is. Long ago I discovered that I can only teach the way that I play.

If you're new to playing the dulcimer, spend some time with this chapter and the exercises and tunes to get your muscles and brain working together. You need to develop patterns that will become automatic, so that as the difficulty of the pieces increases, you'll have muscle memory to rely on. You may find that you'll make some changes to my suggestions, but give my way a good try first. If your body or hands insist that you do something other than what I do, that's okay – but be consistent.

---

[1] More about modes in Book 2.

If you've been playing for some time, parts of this chapter may seem very easy to you, and you may be tempted to breeze through. That may be appropriate, but do spend some time here anyway. If you've developed patterns that you decide you'd like to change, you may find that you'll need to put more energy into relearning new habits than if you were starting from scratch (Oh, you didn't want to hear that!).

Here are two experiments to try:
- Put a left finger down behind any fret (just to the left of the fret), as shown in the photo on the right, below. Press down and pluck the string with any right hand finger. You'll hear a clear tone. Now move your left finger to the middle of the same fret space. Pluck it again. You may still hear a clear tone – it depends on your instrument. Move your left finger further still, as far as you can go within that fret space – as shown in the photo on the left, below. Pluck the string. It will buzz. That's one reason why you want to stay as close behind the fret as possible.
- Put your finger down behind any fret again. Press down hard and play it. Let up the pressure a little bit and play it. Continue reducing the pressure until the string buzzes. Now exert just enough pressure to make the tone clear. Move your finger left, to the center of the fret space and exert the same pressure that gave you a clear tone. It's likely that the string will buzz; you'll need to press down harder in the middle of the fret space, making it more difficult to play. So keep as far to the right in the fret space as possible.

Here, the string will buzz – guaranteed…   *Best tone here!*

Got it? Good.

I've never had a beginning student who didn't want to play all the left hand notes with one finger. Try this: hold out your index finger and move it in the air as if you were playing the piano – up and down the scale. Notice that you are essentially using your arm to make the movement. Now do the same thing, but use your ring finger, middle finger and your index finger. Notice that you are now using your fingers, one after the other, instead of your whole arm. Using fingers is faster and makes everything more fluid. That's what you're after.

If you find that the tips of your fingers hurt, that's because you haven't built up any callus. You will as you play. Assuming that your instrument is set up well and has the correct gauge strings, playing dulcimer doesn't create "mega-callus" – just enough so that your fingers don't hurt.

If you experience pain of any kind, pull back a little. Practice for shorter periods of time. If it continues or gets worse, examine how you're holding the instrument, and your body relative to it. Still bad? Find a teacher who can watch you and help you discover what you need to do differently. Playing should not be painful.

What is tablature and how do I read it?

Ready to start playing? Let's begin with "First Things #1" (below). What you're seeing is basic tablature (or TAB) for dulcimer. On the top you have a familiar looking musical staff. Below that are three lines that say "string 1, string 2, string 3."   String one is always the one closest to you. If you're playing a four-string dulcimer with the first two strings close together, then those unisons are regarded as "string 1." These three lines are just as if you are looking down at the fretboard – every line represents a string. Think of it as a sort of aerial view of the instrument.

If, like me, you're playing a four-string instrument where all four strings are equidistant, then, in terms of reading TAB, you ignore the second string for now. It takes some getting used to, but it will become automatic as you learn to read tablature better. That open second string will create a wonderful drone – sometimes dissonant, but to my ears that drone brings back a traditional sound to the instrument, even if we're not playing strictly in the traditional style.

Here's what I mean:

```
3 ________________________________
2 ________________________________
drone ________________________
1 ________________________________
```

In this first exercise, you're only playing on the first string with both your left hand and your right hand – one thing at a time. Is it obvious that "i" is for index finger and "r" for is ring finger of your left hand? Good. Soon you'll be playing "m" for middle, and later on you'll find "t" for thumb and the occasional "p" for pinkie. The numbers on the TAB lines (0, 1, 2) refer to what fret you'll be playing, with 0 being an open string.

Try playing "First Things #1," paying attention to the suggested fingering for your left hand. (Don't forget the speaker icons that lead you to recorded versions of the exercises and tunes – see page 7.) The "C" in the first measure of the notation is another way of writing 4/4 time.

Track 1

You may have noticed that I had you start with the ring finger of your left hand, so that you have fingers to spare as you go up the fretboard. When you come down again, you start with your index finger for the same reason – you don't want to run out of fingers! By the way, "up the fretboard" is away from the tuners and toward your right hand. You'll probably think it should be the other way around. Get used to this one – up is always from the left to the right on any fretted instrument. Think of it in terms of the notes going higher, or up the scale as you move up the fretboard.

In "First Things #2," you'll notice a slur with the word "transfer" [2] under it. When you are going up or down the fretboard, at some point you *will* run out of fingers and you have to figure out a way to keep going. In measure #6, as you're moving down, you run out of usable fingers when your ring finger arrives at the 2nd fret.[3] While you're playing that next open note, you have time to exchange your ring finger with your index finger. Now you have your ring finger free to continue down to the 1st fret. This concept should be familiar to those of you with a background in piano or guitar.

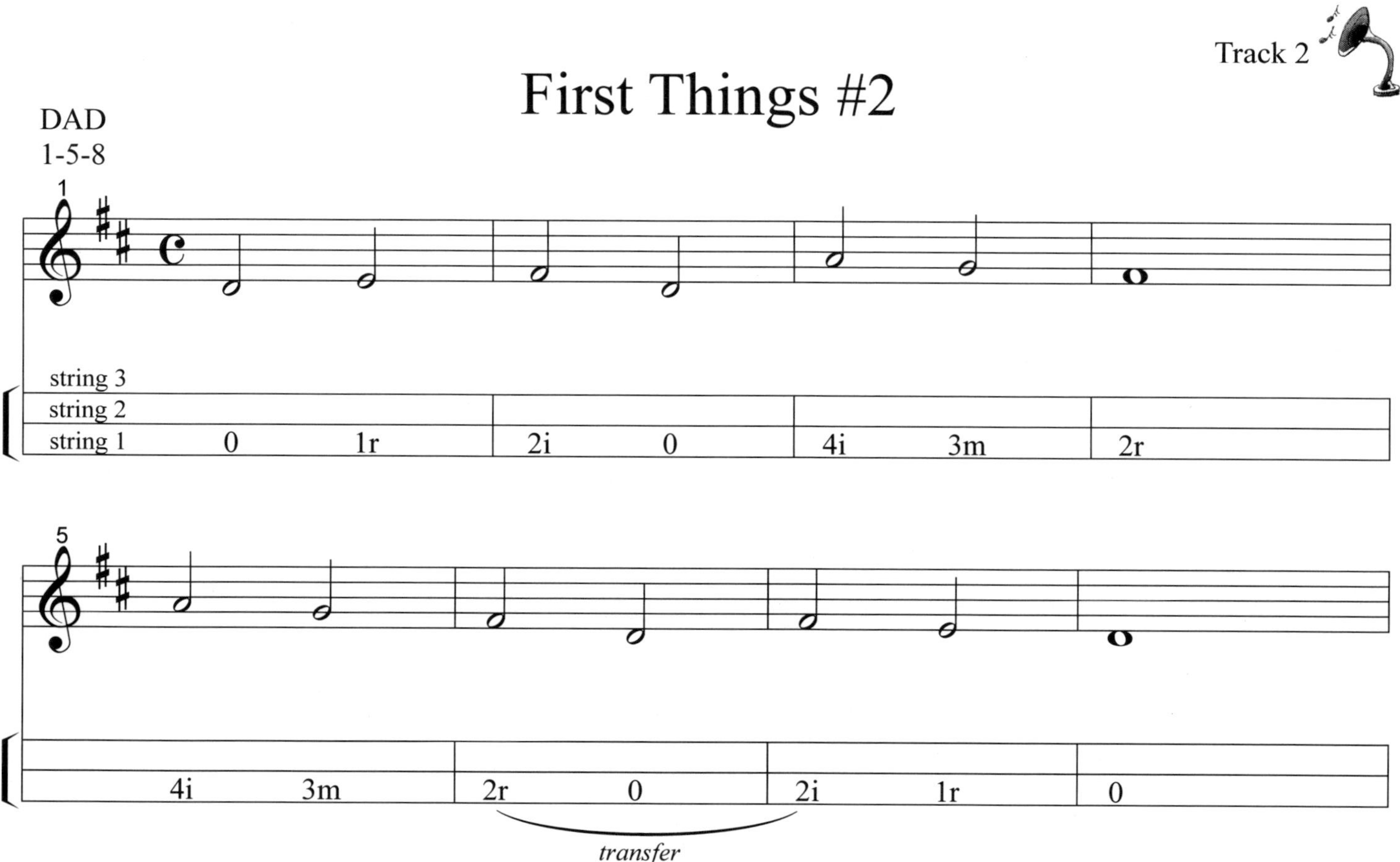

Practice this fingering a bunch of times, until it feels automatic. Then go on to "First Things #3." Same left hand pattern, except this time you strum all the way across with your right hand. Check yourself to make sure you haven't altered the fingering.

---

[2] "Transfer" is my own term. You won't find it used in other books.

[3] We're not using the pinkie at this point.

An important reminder: because I play with four equidistant strings, sometimes you'll hear my open drone string ringing through in the audio files, especially when I'm strumming, as in "First Things #3." If you're playing with a three-string setup, don't let that confuse you.

First Things #3

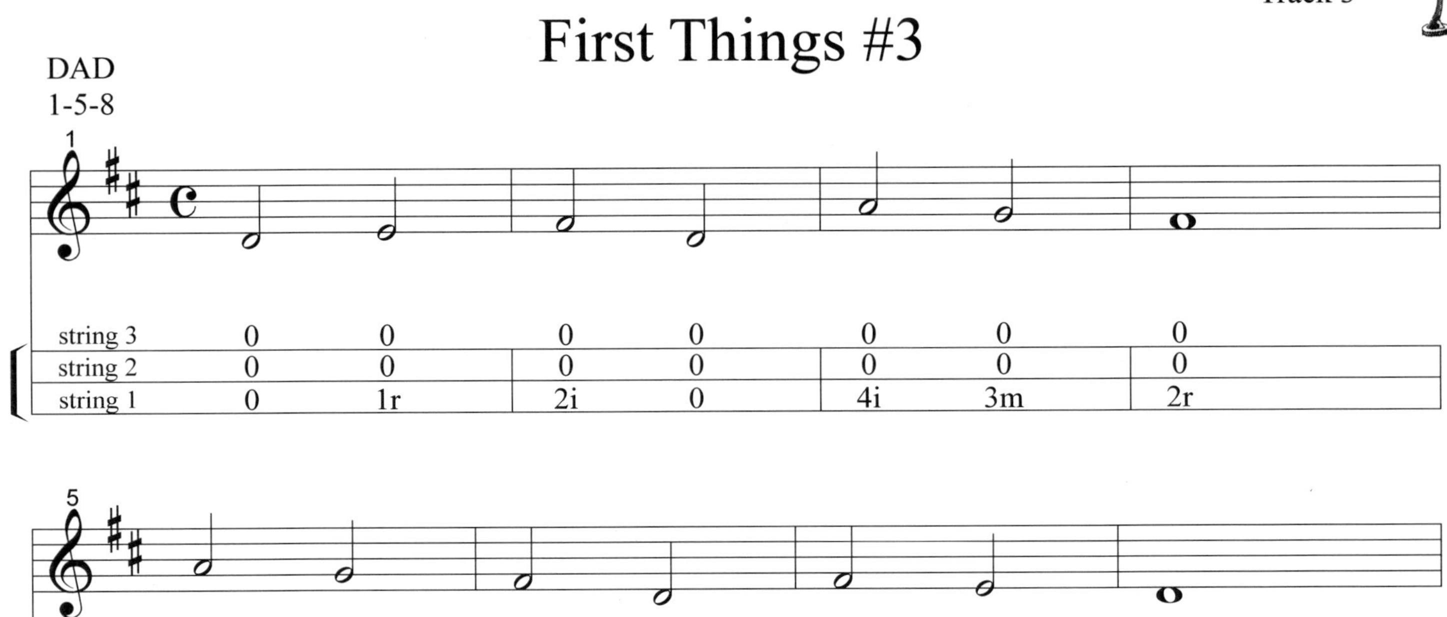

So now you've got the idea of progressive and consistent fingering and you understand the concept of transferring fingers.

Here's another exercise. It's the same idea, except this time you transfer without an open note between the two notes. You just have to move a little faster. Play as slowly as you need to, keeping your speed consistent. You don't want to speed up for the easier sections and then have to slow down for the more difficult parts. Try to keep a regular beat.

Take a look at "First Things #4." In the first two lines you play only on the first string. Once you get a handle on the fingering, move on to the last two lines where the melody and the fingering are the same as before, but you're strumming across all your strings.

Continue playing these pieces until you get sufficiently comfortable to move on. Keep in mind that you need to get the basics of left hand fingering down before you go to the next chapter, but you don't need to be perfect. You'll be reinforcing this lesson with each new thing you try. Just check in with yourself every once in a while to make sure you haven't slipped into "creative" fingering.

As you work through this book you will notice that I don't use my left pinkie very often. My little finger bends inwardly quite dramatically, and therefore I lose a lot of the stretch between my ring finger and pinkie. It also doesn't come down directly, flat on the fretboard, so I tend to favor my thumb and other three fingers. If using your little finger feels comfortable to you, then you've got one more finger to use. Absolutely use it – you're one step ahead of the game. Just alter fingering as you see fit.

Mary had… something familiar

Many of the tunes and exercises in this book are original, but every once in a while I'll give you a "touchstone," something familiar that will enable you to make sure that you're doing things correctly. As you play "Mary Had a Little Lamb," pay close attention to the fingering, and strum all the way across the strings. Keep your hands relaxed and "in the position," and maintain pressure on the string until you need to move, so that you get a smooth transition to the next note. Check your fingering to make sure that you stay as close behind each fret as possible. If you hear buzzes, it's likely that your fingers have strayed to... somewhere else!

You'll notice that there is no accompanying music file with this tune. I couldn't bring myself to record it… you *know* how this song goes! In fact, try playing it first just by ear, without the TAB! Start on the 2nd fret and see how you do. Sneaking a peak is allowed.

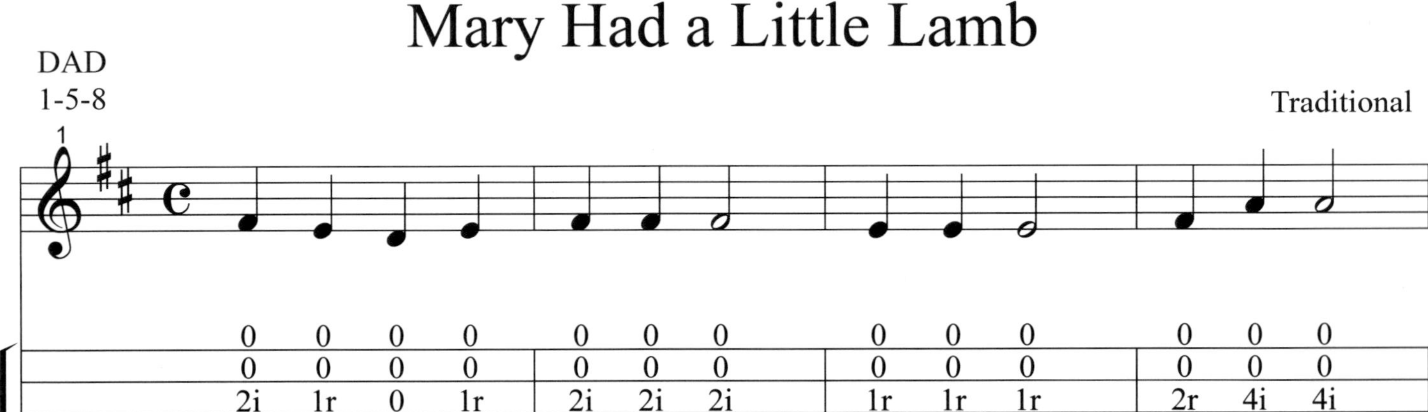

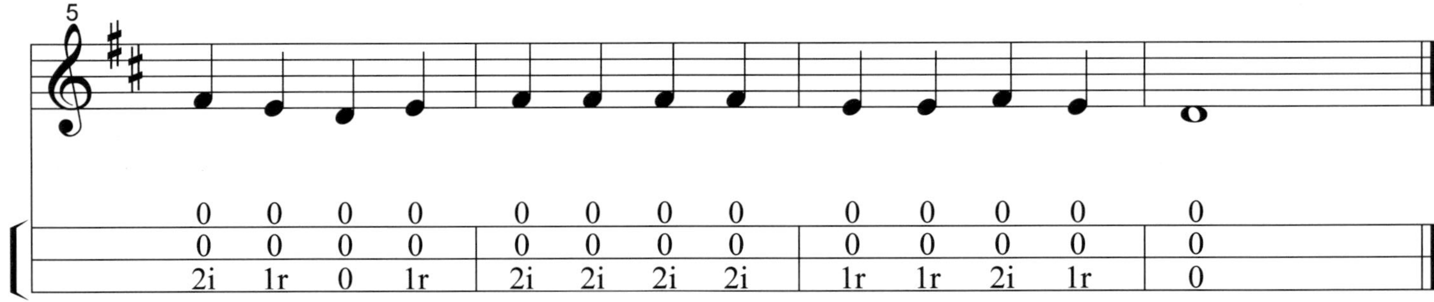

"First Tune" and "Second Tune"

You may not find yourself humming "First Tune" and "Second Tune" while you make dinner, but these two tunes will help you reinforce the basic skills you've learned in this chapter!

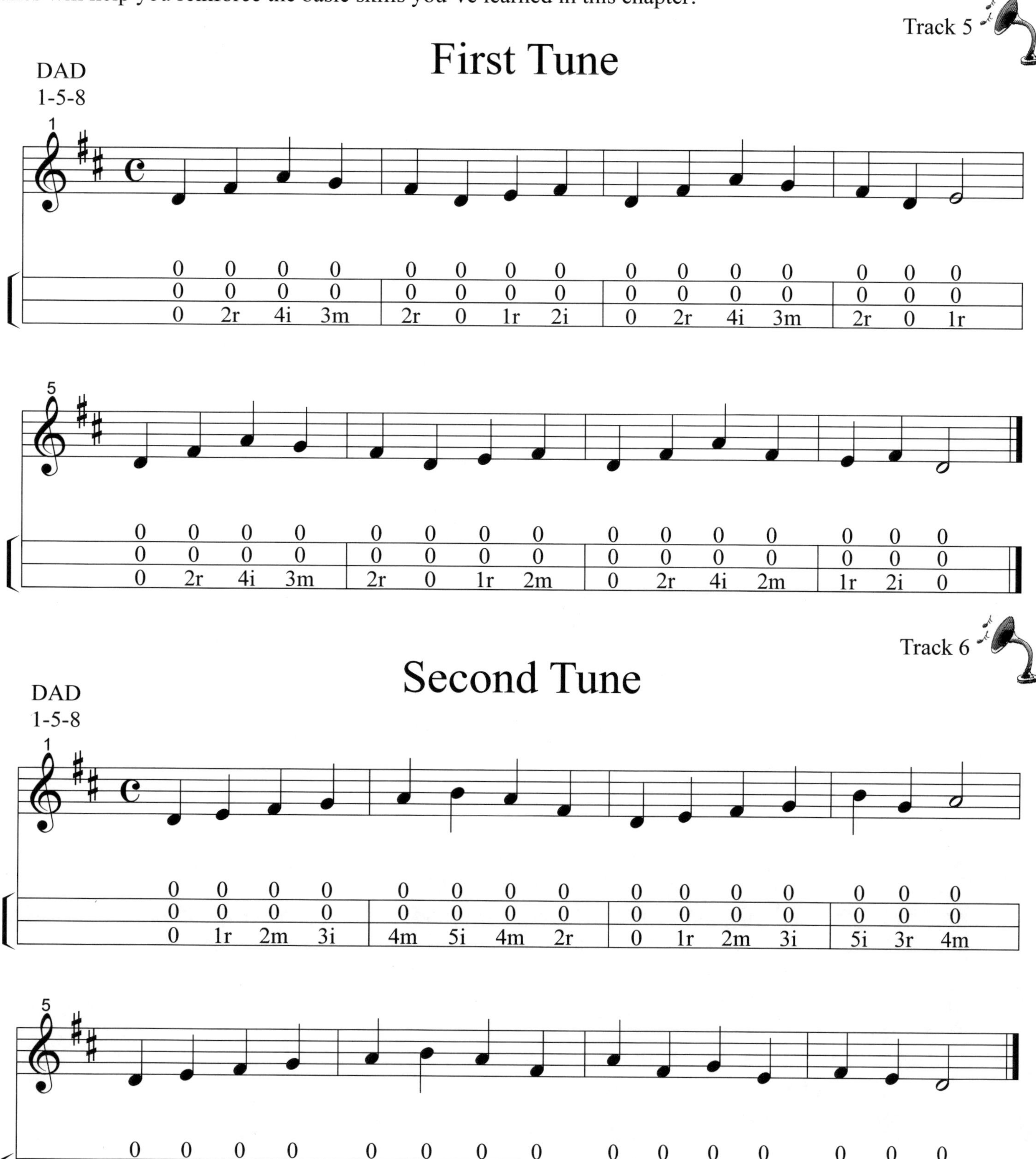

There you have it – you've got a foundation in basic fingering for both hands. But before we go on, I want you to do yourself a big favor. Flip back to "First Things #1." Review it and then play it without looking at the music. Do the same with "First Things #2 - #4," "First Tune" and "Second Tune." Reviewing chapters and "getting off the paper" is a great habit to cultivate.

Chapter 2 ~ Recognizing Frets

Technically, the fret is the wire bar itself, not the spaces between the frets. Common usage, however, lets us use the term "fret" to define both the actual bar *and* the space directly to its left.

How to find your way around the fretboard

Any time you read tablature or are being shown how to play something on the dulcimer, you have to know what fret you're being asked to play. If I were to ask you to play something on the 1st fret, that would be easy. But if I ask you to find the 6th fret, it's likely that you'd start counting up from the 1st fret to find it. This chapter will help you learn how to recognize any fret quickly and efficiently.

If you've gotten this far without a 6½ fret, I congratulate you on your tenacity. Now go out and get a 6½ fret installed on your dulcimer. You'll need it to effectively use this book.

Here again is the fretboard layout. This time it's only for dulcimers with the 6½ fret, and I'm only showing you three strings. *Four-string equidistant players, remember that your second string is a free floating drone and you read three-string TAB by playing your first, third and fourth strings.*

1		2	3		4		5	6	6½	7		8		9	10

We all process information differently. I'm going to show you the way that I look at the fretboard – you may find that you'll develop your own techniques for finding frets. My goal here is to start you thinking in terms of recognizing frets without counting up from the 1st fret. If you find another technique that makes more sense to you, go for it.

The 1st and 2nd frets are easy. They're just the first two frets closest to the headstock, and they're both big frets. Now, sight in the next fret – notice how it's a little fret? That's your 3rd fret. Play any string on the 3rd fret a few times, and as you do it, say, *out loud*, "third fret, third fret, third fret," or even "three, three, three." Now, just to be thorough, go back and do the same thing for the 1st and 2nd fret. Press down just behind the fret itself and say its number out loud as you play it.

The frets that people tend to recognize less easily are those above the 3rd fret. Here's how I think of it. Skip up to the 6th, 6½ and 7th frets. Notice how those three frets create a "cluster." They are three small frets, all close together. The 7th fret, which is the octave (same note as your open string, but an octave higher), is the little fret farthest to the right in the cluster. Press down just behind the 7th fret and say, *out loud*, "seven, seven, seven." Now go back to the 6th fret, which you've probably already sighted in as the first in the cluster of three close-together frets. Repeat the "out loud" exercise.

Now, finding the 6½ fret is simple – it's the one in the middle of the cluster. Right? Again, repeat your mantra for the 6½ fret.

I don't spend a lot of time playing above the 7th fret and I hardly ever fret above the 10th. But it's a good idea to get well acquainted with the frets up to the 10th. Look to the right of the "cluster." You've got a big fret, another big fret and then a little fret. That little fret is your 10th fret. The 8th and 9th will fall into place in your mind as you get to recognize the "cluster" and the 10th fret. Press down behind each of those frets, say the number out loud – you know the routine.

Now all we've got left are the 4th and 5th frets. The 5th is easy, as it's a big fret, just to the left of the "cluster." Sight in the 3rd and 5th frets – there's your 4th fret, lurking between them. Practice your mantra for the 4th and 5th frets.

Some instrument makers build in visual cues to help you. One of my students has white dots inlaid into the fretboard on the 3rd, 7th, 10th and 14th frets. My standard *Blue Lion* has a rose inlay that snakes from the 5th to the 7th. My bass dulcimer has dots at the 3rd, 7th and 14th (the 14th being the second octave).

Your instrument may or may not have dots or inlays, but if you have them, use them to recognize where you are on the fretboard. If you don't have any cues built in to your dulcimer, you might find it helpful to put a piece of tape or a sticky label on the 3rd and 7th frets. However, the fact that dulcimers have differently spaced frets is probably the single most helpful piece of information.

If somewhere down the pike you catch yourself counting to find a fret, go back and practice finding that fret with whatever "immediate recognition" method makes sense to you. Being able to move quickly and reliably to any fret is just one of many methods that can help streamline your playing.

Chapter 3 ~ Basic Right Hand Techniques

Flat-picking, strumming, picking and plucking

This chapter is an introduction to right hand technique. Most of you will be playing a three-string dulcimer (remember: that can be either a dulcimer that is set up with three equidistant strings, or a four-string dulcimer set up with the first two strings close together, effectively making those two strings a single string). The following instruction will work for either three-string or four-string equidistant setups.

Remember: if you're playing with four equidistant strings, anything that is specific to you will be written in italics. As usual, your second string will be a "floating" string – a drone you let ring out as an open string when you are strumming and that you can ignore when you are fingerpicking. It might help to pretend that your second string doesn't exist! This may confuse you and make you wonder why I bother to recommend four equidistant strings. Hang tight – when we get to the chapter on Advanced Right Hand Technique in Book 2, you're going to be so glad *that you have that string!*

You may notice that I repeat myself quite often in this chapter. That's because I've taught enough to know how often people need to be reminded about fingering. Think of it more as nagging.

For the sake of clarity, we're going to define three different things that you can do with your right hand:
- Strumming is, well, strumming; brush across all your strings, either toward you or away from you. It can be done with a flat pick, with your thumb or with a finger. I use all three methods, but my "default" is to strum toward myself with my index finger.
- Picking is when you play one string at a time using your thumb on the first string *(and second string for four-string players)* and your index and/or middle finger(s) on your two lowest strings.
- Plucking is when you pick up more than one string at a time and play them together. [1]

Strumming, flat picks, shoulders, arms, fingers and where to play

Traditionally, mountain dulcimers were strummed more than picked or plucked. Often the quill end of a feather was used instead of a pick. These days people tend to use a flat pick. I fingerpick more than I strum – that's just my style – but if you think you might like using a pick, here are some hints that might help you.

In the chapter about basics, I mentioned that many people start out with a big, on-the-soft-side flat pick and eventually graduate to a smaller, harder pick, which gives you more control. Think about the big, fat pencils you used in first grade. They were very helpful when you were learning the crude motions involved with writing. But imagine using one of those pencils now, having learned the fine motor skills of writing.

Find a pick that feels good in your hands. It can't hurt to start out with a small, hard pick and see if it feels comfortable. I like a nylon, .88 mm pick made by Jim Dunlop. The medium gray ones. They're a little rough at the top, which makes them easier to hang on to. On the opposite end of the spectrum, I've seen people make big flat picks out of a plastic milk jug.

---

[1] In chapter 1, plucking was described as the action of picking a single string. However, in this chapter and the three that follow, the word "pluck" refers to the action of two or more strings played together.

Whatever pick you decide to start with, hold it between your thumb and the tips of your index and middle fingers.[2] Keep your fingers relaxed. Although your wrist does move with the motion of the strumming, most of the action comes from your forearm. Make sure that your right shoulder doesn't rise up (keep your shoulder out of your ear, please).

When using fingers instead of a pick, most people's inclination is to strum away with their thumbs. The thumb creates a nice floppy sound – good for some things, but in general I like the more precise sound created by the nail of the index finger. Using your index finger, you get the nail sound when you strum away and the pad of your index finger when you come back. It provides a nice contrast. Experiment with those different ideas.

To the right end of your instrument, between the highest fret and the saddle, there should be a carved out section of the fretboard. Most people assume that you should strum there. Go ahead and strum across the strings as far to the right as you can. Most instruments sound very brittle there. Now move your strumming to the left and experiment with how it sounds. Go all the way to the 7th fret. All instruments are different, but in general the closer you get to the middle of the fretboard the warmer the sound will be. You may also notice that your right arm falls in its most comfortable, relaxed position somewhere around the 8th or 9th fret.

That is where I tend to play. If my left hand is fretting above the 7th fret, I let it chase my right hand further up the fretboard, but when my left hand goes back to the lower frets, my right hand comes back to settle around the middle of the instrument. It may be different for you, your body, your instrument, but the main thing to know is that you don't have to play at the cut-out, unless you particularly like that sound or want to use it to embellish a particular tune or section of a tune.

If you like the sound you get playing over the carved out section, or it feels comfortable to you to play there, make very, very sure that your right shoulder stays down.

Strumming – your turn

In these first exercises you're going to be using only your right hand – one thing at a time. Before you move on to specific exercises, just fool around with the flat pick or your index finger, strumming in such a way that you're playing all the strings with equal volume. Try this:
- Strum away from your body.
- Strum back.
- Combine strumming away and strumming back.
- Experiment: strum away three times, strum back one, change the rhythm. Go wild!

---

[2] This is different from flat-picking a guitar, where you fold your index finger down and hold the pick between your thumb and flat edge of your index finger. If you play guitar and are used to playing that way, experiment and see what works best for you.

When you've had enough fun with that, play the following exercises. The arrows indicate which way you're strumming. Continuing to use your index finger or a pick – whichever feels best to you – repeat until just *before* you start screaming.

Strumming #1

DAD
1-5-8

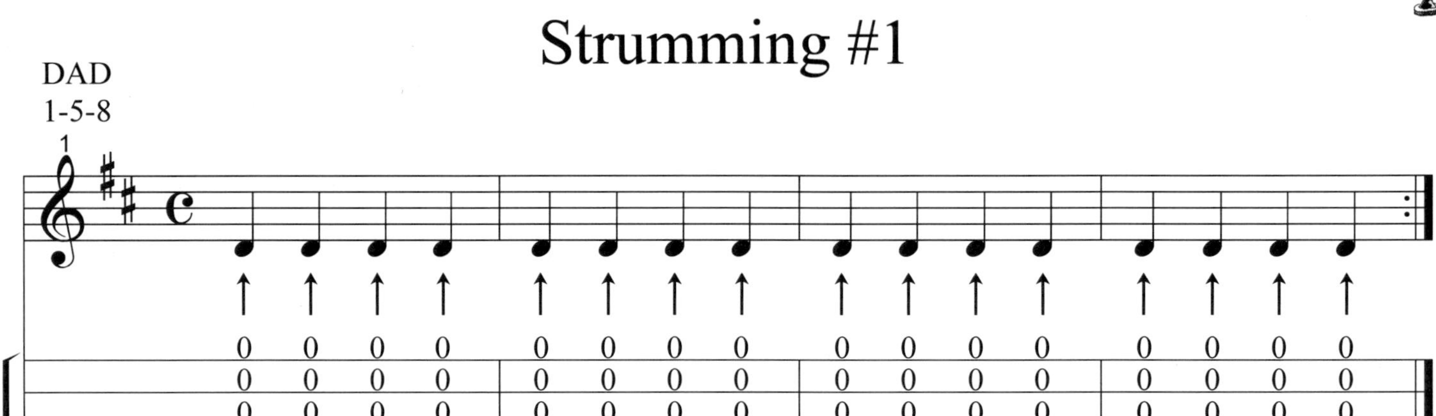

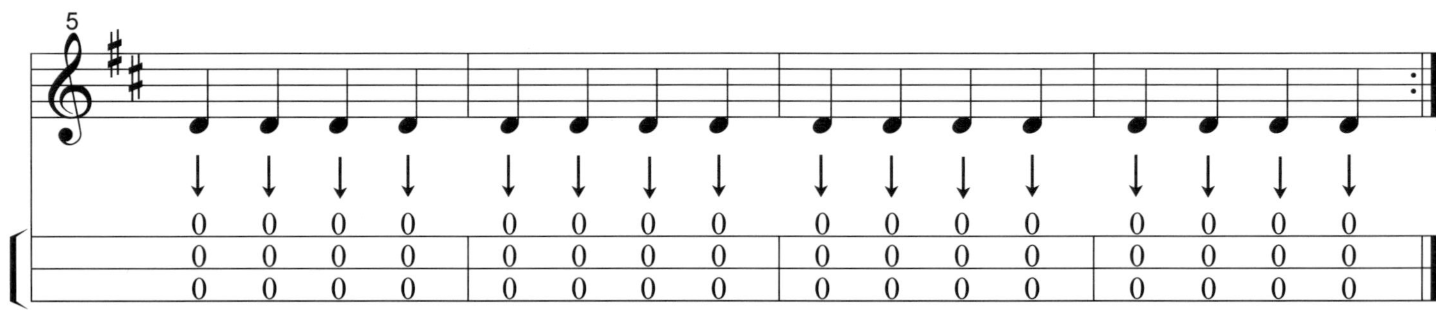

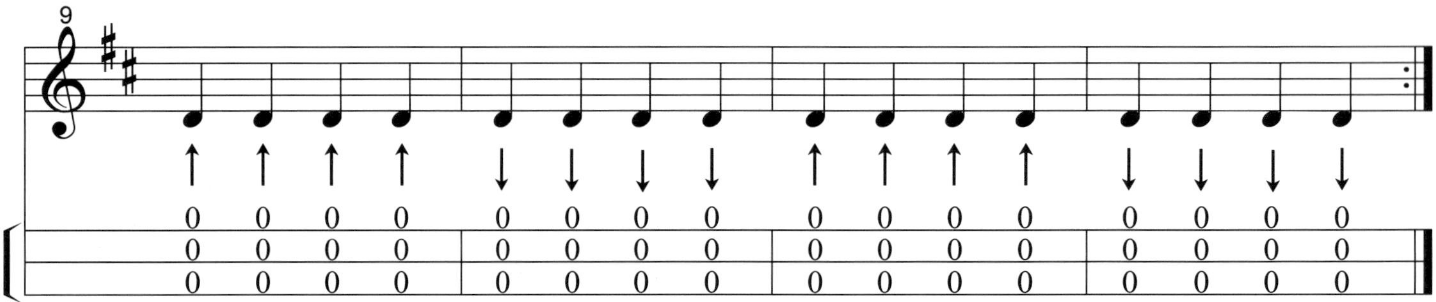

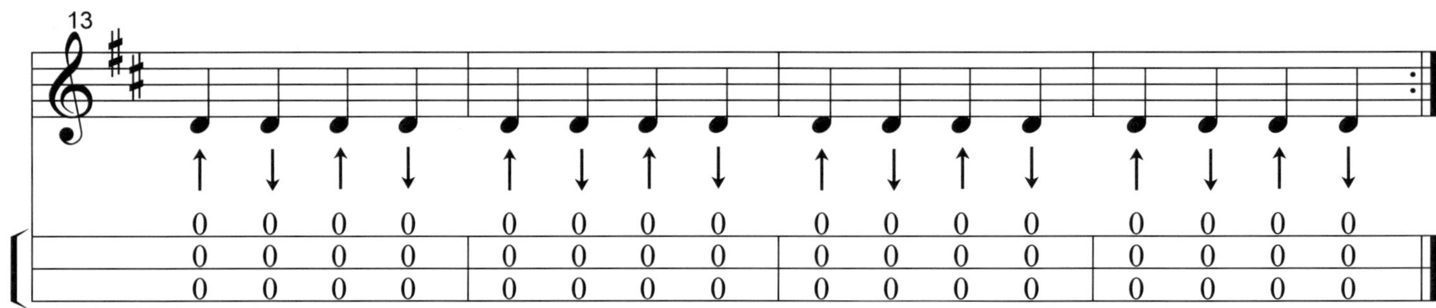

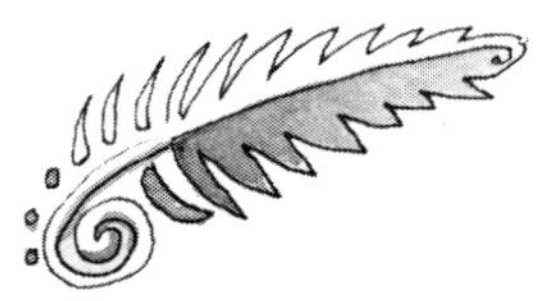

Here's a pattern in 4/4 time where each measure ends on a half note. That will give you a little time to think between measures. The transition between measures can be a challenge. Getting your brain to tell your hand to go, "away, back, away" and then "away, back, away" again can take some time. Be patient.

Strumming #2

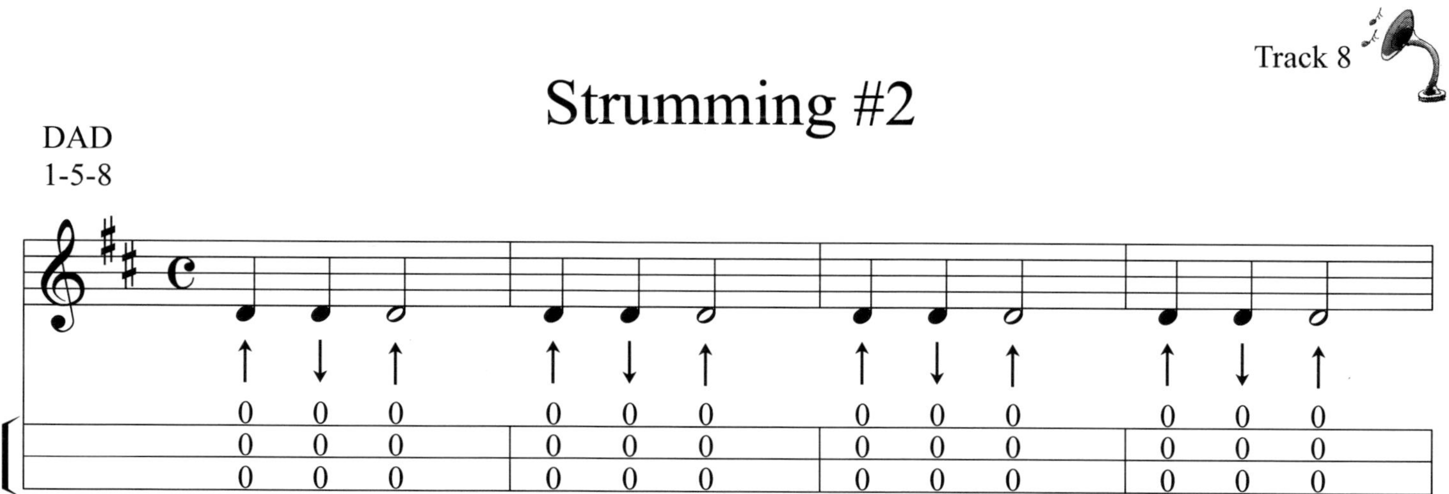

The next pattern is similar to "Strumming #2," except now there are only three beats in a measure (3/4 time). You don't have the luxury of the extra beat between the end of one measure and the beginning of the next – you've got to be ready for the next "away." It might help to think in terms of accenting the first beat of each measure.

Strumming #3

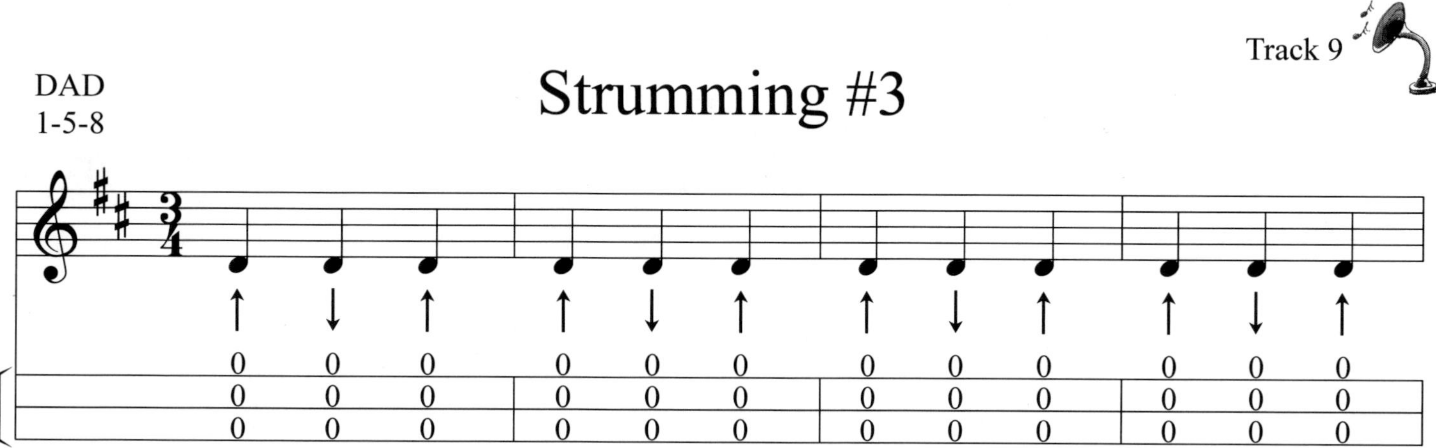

The following is a traditional strumming pattern. You hear it used so often in tunes like "Old Joe Clark" or "Boil Them Cabbage Down" that it has a nickname. It gets dubbed "bum-did-dee," and sounds a little like a galloping horse. Do you remember the beginning of the theme to "Bonanza?" Then you've got it. Count out the beats before you begin.

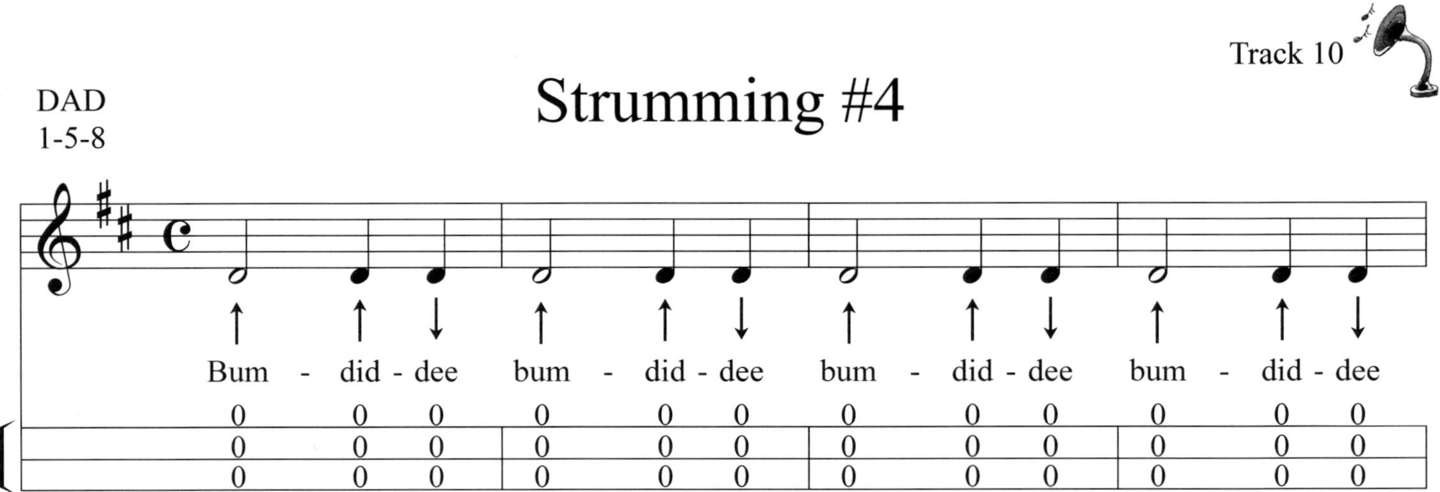

There are endless ways to combine these patterns. Once you feel you've got a handle on the exercises we just did, and have played around with some of your own ideas, it's time to bring your left hand into the picture. For "The Twinkle Opus," work slowly and remember to laugh if your left hand and your right hand seem to not quite agree on what they're trying to do. You're doing the equivalent of patting your head and rubbing your tummy.

Keep an eye out for the following changes:
- Fingering
- Timing
- Direction of strum

When you get to the final line, play the timing for each measure as indicated, keeping your right hand moving through the "bum-did-dee" pattern.

The first three lines (systems) will take care of themselves, but when you get to the last system (measures #13-#16), you have extra "bum-did-dee" strums that can bury the melody. See if you can emphasize the melody notes by playing them a little louder and letting all the other strums (the *uhs*) be light and in the background.

The Twinkle Opus

DAD
1-5-8

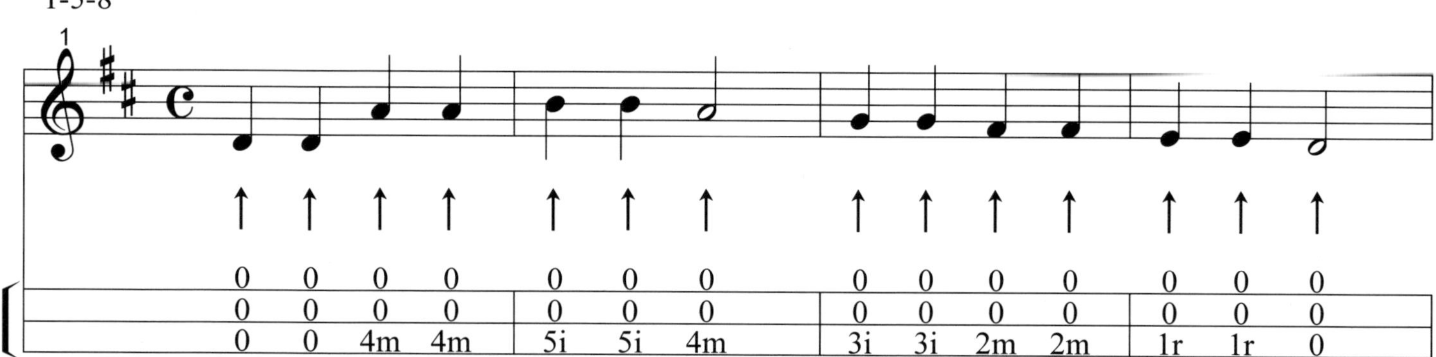

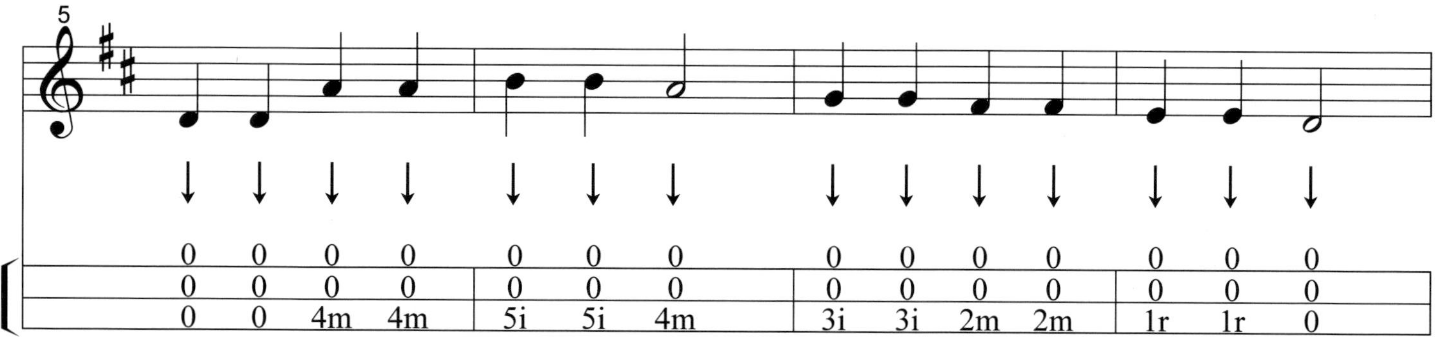

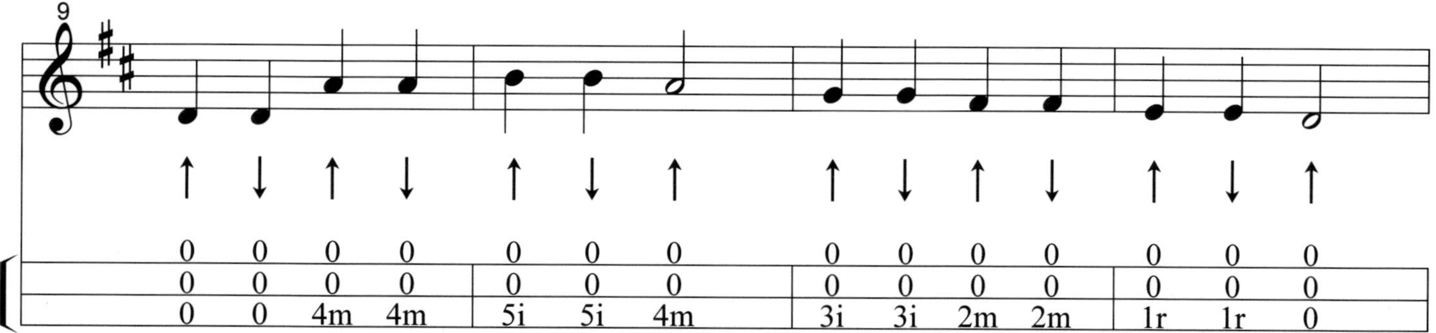

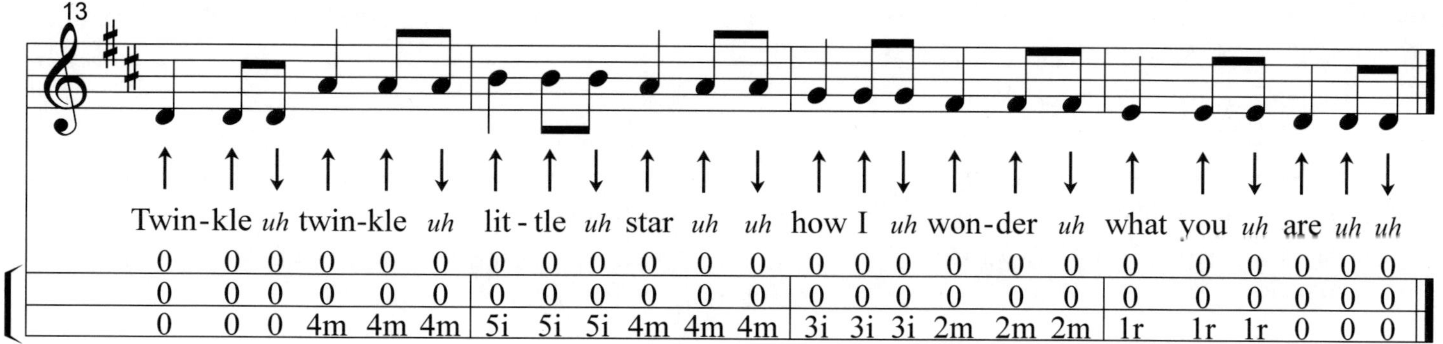

How did you do? That pattern can take a while to coordinate.

To get a little more practice with "bum-did-dee," try playing the first line of the old tune "Old Blue."

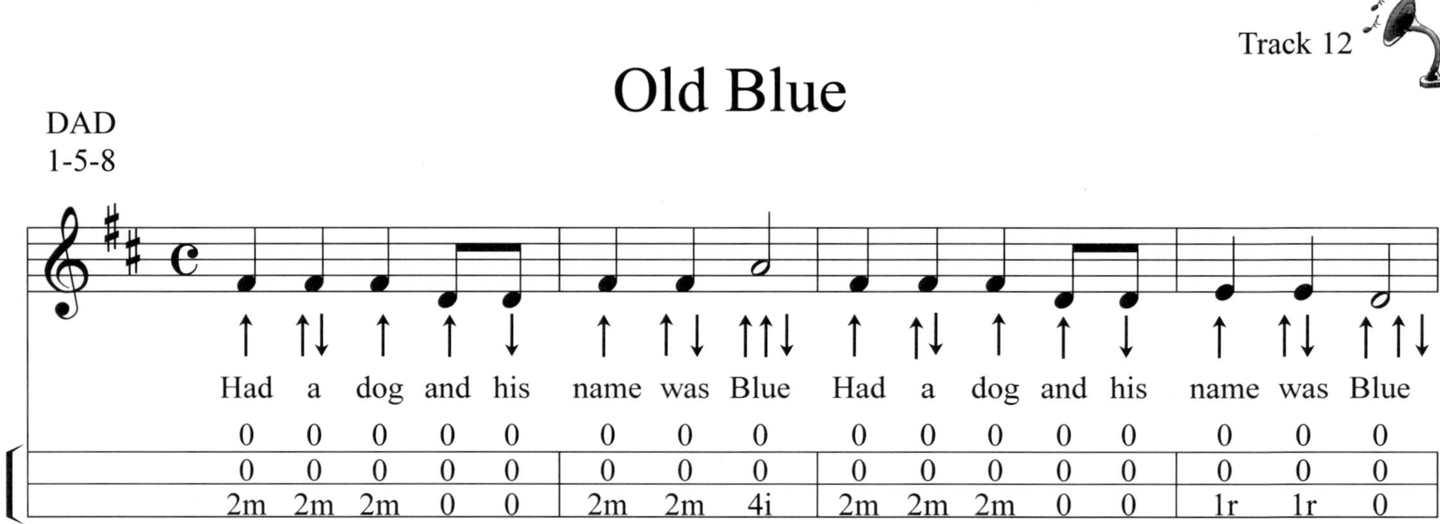

If this whole concept is giving you trouble, let's see if I can help clarify what your right hand is doing. The words to the musical line you just played are: "Had a dog and his name was Blue."

But what your right hand is actually doing, if you're playing the "bum-did-dee's" correctly, would be this:

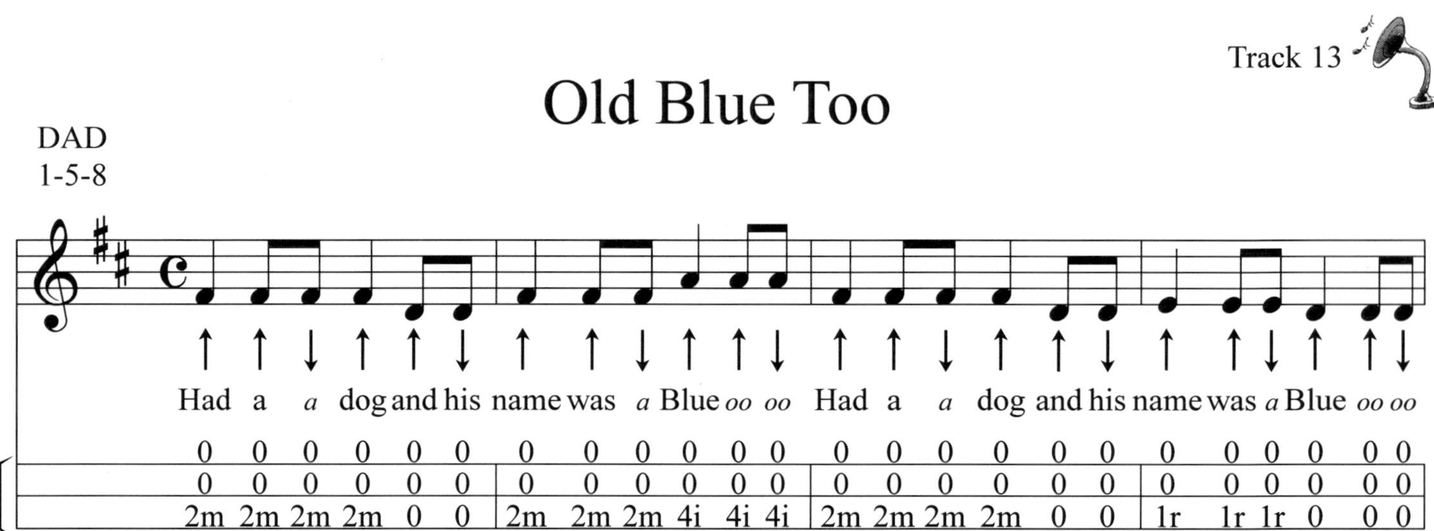

Saying the lyrics out loud while you play may help your brain and your right hand work together (and what could be more fun than getting to sing, "Blue-oo-oo?"). The real joy of playing the "bum-did-dee" pattern is that, with time, it becomes natural and you can speed it up. Practice it every once in a while and it will eventually get into your right hand.

There you have it for basic strumming techniques. You might not find a place to use these patterns right away, but I suspect you'll find that they'll creep up on you and you'll discover yourself using them in your playing. Experimentation will tell you if you should be using your fingers or a pick for strumming. You often get more drive to your playing with a pick, but I generally prefer the gentler sound of just fingers.

Fingerpicking patterns

Now, we move on to fingerpicking. You have a choice to make at this point. I almost always use the thumb of my right hand to pick the first string. *I also use it on my second string, because I play with four equidistant strings.* The choice you have to make is what finger/fingers you use to play the two lowest strings. Despite all my insistence that you go for consistency in whatever you do, this is one place where I don't always do it the same way. If you've been using a flat pick for the strumming exercises, now is the time to get rid of it and just use your fingers.

The logical way to play the bottom two strings would be to use your middle finger (we're talking right hand here – right?) on the bass string and your index finger on the middle string. I often do that. But sometimes (true confessions here) I let my index finger run both lower strings. There will be times when you're plucking more than one string at once (but not strumming) when you'll need all three *(or even four)* fingers at once.

So in the following exercises, I'm not going to specify which right-hand fingers you use. Experiment and find what works best for you. I would suggest, however, that you do use your thumb on the first string. I would *more* than suggest that.

As we did with strumming, we're going to start out only using your right hand. Here's the first thing to try, which gives you two quarter notes and then a half note. That gives you time to think as you make the transition from one measure to the next. Remember, you're using either your index finger, or your middle and index fingers to run your two lowest strings, and your thumb on the first string *(four-string equidistant players, remember to ignore your second string)*.

These notes are not being played together, but are in sequence – one after the other.

Track 14

Fingerpicking #1

DAD
1-5-8

Now try the same thing, but in 3/4 time, making a faster transition from one measure to the next.

Track 15

Fingerpicking #2

DAD
1-5-8

Next up is a "pluck": you play more than one string at the same time *(four-string equidistant players, just pretend that second string doesn't exist).* It looks the same in the TAB whether you are plucking or strumming. The only indicator that you're supposed to be plucking instead of strumming is that I'm telling you so, although I often insert "direction of strum" arrows if I'm indicating a strum. Unless I specify plucking or strumming, use either at your own discretion.

For the pluck, use your thumb, middle and index finger to gently play all three strings with equal volume; don't let your arm come into the picture (well, you can let it support your hand but don't let it "flail" – there will be no flailing, please).

Your job here will be to make the pluck controlled and even, so that one string doesn't sound louder than another. There will come a time when you may want to make a note – say, the melody of a tune – sound stronger than other notes, but that's not now.

Track 16

Fingerpicking #3

DAD
1-5-8

Not too bad, right? Now we're going to combine some of these elements. The pattern will be pick, pluck.

Track 17

Fingerpicking #4

DAD
1-5-8

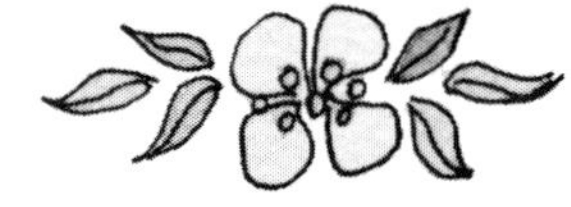

And why not try it as a waltz in 3/4 time? This time it's pick, pluck, pluck.

Fingerpicking #5

You can combine picking and plucking, as in this next exercise. Notice that we've moved back to 4/4 timing.

Fingerpicking #6

You can also combine strumming and picking. For the first note use your middle or index finger, for the second note strum with your index finger, and then let your thumb pick up the last two notes.

Fingerpicking #7

When you strum across, one minor adjustment that you can make is to choose *not* to strum the bass string. When you get going with these patterns, I suspect you'll find that you actually play it more like this:

Fingerpicking #8

And, of course, you can always combine picking, plucking and strumming. Remember, for the sake of these exercises, that when you've got more than one note to play at one time, you strum if there's an arrow indicating the direction of the strum and you pluck if there is no arrow. (In later chapters if I don't make that clear, then it's up to you whether you strum or pluck.)

For this exercise, you pick, strum, pick, pluck. Got that?

Fingerpicking #9

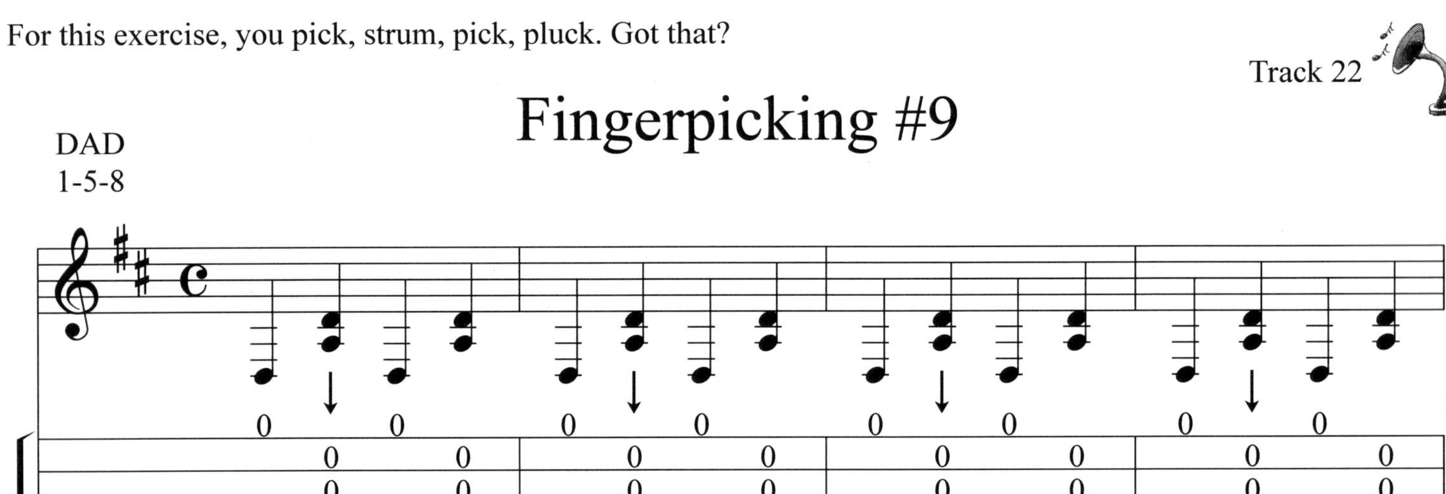

Getting comfortable with your right hand? If so, it's time to bring in your left hand. No arrows? Ah, you must be plucking. Your right hand pattern would be pick (with your index or middle finger) and then pluck (with your thumb and index finger). Do that pattern twice per measure. The indicated fingering is for your *left* hand.

Fingerpicking #10

You've just added a new ball to your juggling. Spend some time with this new concept if it doesn't come naturally to you. Move on to the next exercise only when you feel ready.

"Fingerpicking #11" is basically the same thing you just did, but your right hand is doing the same pattern you did in "Fingerpicking #9" – pick, strum, pick, pluck.

Here's an important clarification for you:

If you glance back at "Fingerpicking #1 - #11," you'll notice that there are musical notes in the staff for each and every TAB designation (i.e. look at "Fingerpicking #11" above. The second notes of the first measure, strummed together, are represented in the TAB by [0,2r]). For these specific exercises I felt it was important to make sure that you understood that when the TAB indicated a multi-note pluck or strum that you were, in fact, playing multiple notes.

However, most of the time when you look at music for the dulcimer, there is only a single note in the music staff (usually the melody), even though the TAB would indicate that you are to play more than one note. Confused? Look ahead to the very first note in the next tune, "Snow In Spring." Do you see how there is a single A note in the music, but the TAB below it (0,0,4) indicates that you are playing a three note chord? Which you are!

Common usage for dulcimer TAB is to write only the melody in the music staff, even if the TAB often indicates that you are actually playing more than a single note. It's less cluttered, and therefore easier to read (and to write!). Unless I'm attempting to clarify something specific (as in the last few exercises), you will see the simplified version in this tutorial and you'll hear that reflected in my playing in the accompanying music files.

How about putting what you've been working on into a tune? (Finally!) "Snow in Spring" brings together picking and strumming. Clap out the rhythm, or at least look it over, before you begin playing.

Pay attention to where you need to transfer your left hand fingering. Let your right index finger handle the strums, and your right thumb handle the individual notes throughout the whole piece. That means (nagging again here) that you *strum* the first notes of every odd-numbered measure and you *pick* all the other notes.

Snow In Spring

©2015 Anne Dodson

DAD
1-5-8

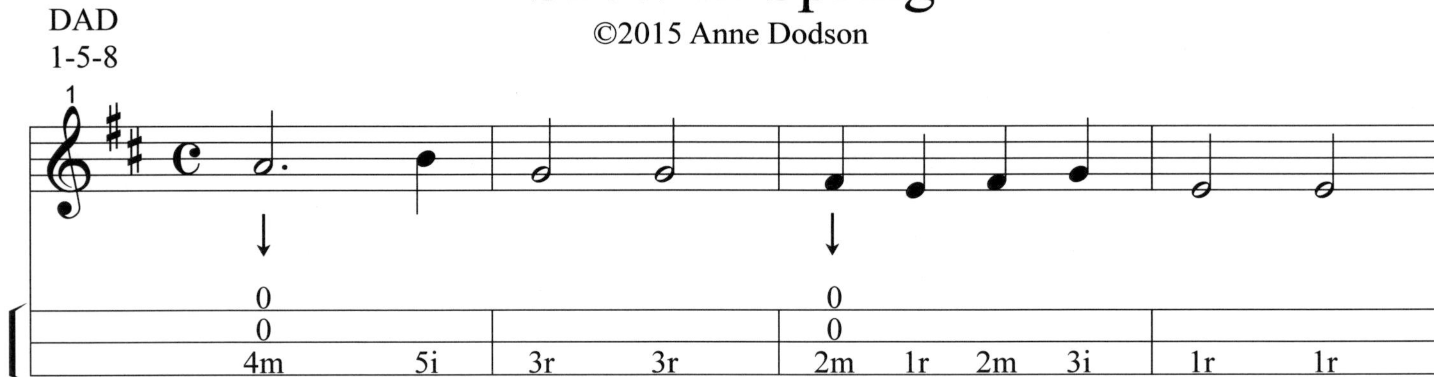

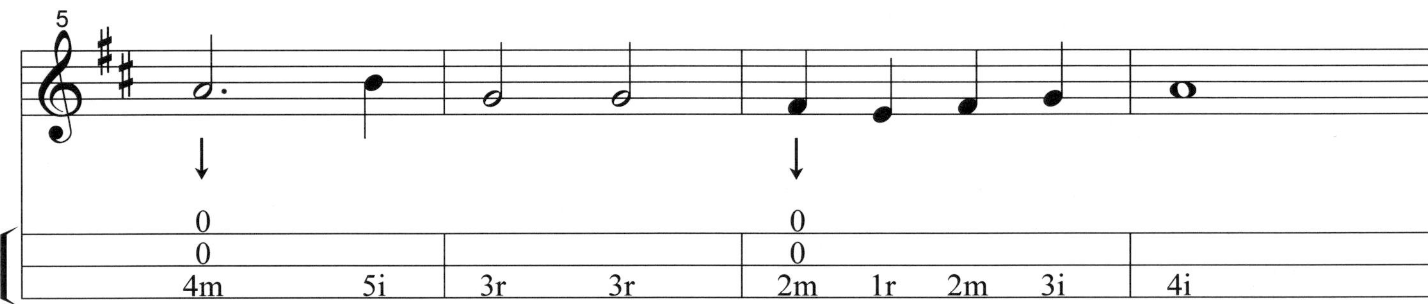

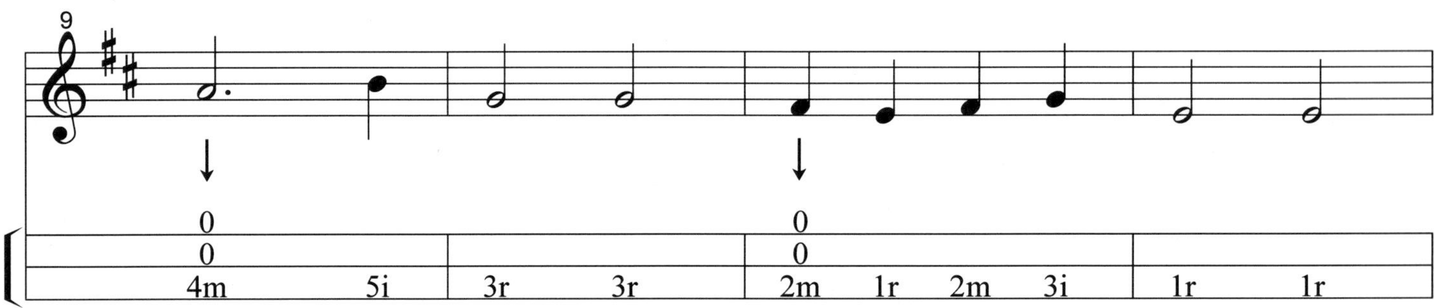

With "Frère Jacques," you add plucking to strumming and picking. Here's your right hand pattern:

1. First line – strum, pick, pluck, pick.
2. Second line – strum, pick, pluck
3. Third line – strum, pick, pick, pick, pluck, pick.
4. Last line – strum, pick, pluck. Notice that I'm asking you to pick your open middle string all by itself – not as part of a pluck. Use your right index finger.

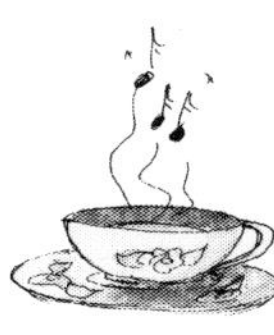

Your brain might fuss at first, asking your fingers to make those changes, especially when you're trying to use your left hand too. It's worth the investment to take it slowly and really get those brain pathways coordinated with your hands. *Remember, you four-string equidistant players, that the string indicated as your middle string in three-string tablature is your* third *string, not your second (unison) string.*

Track 26 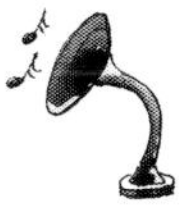

Frère Jacques

DAD
1-5-8

Traditional

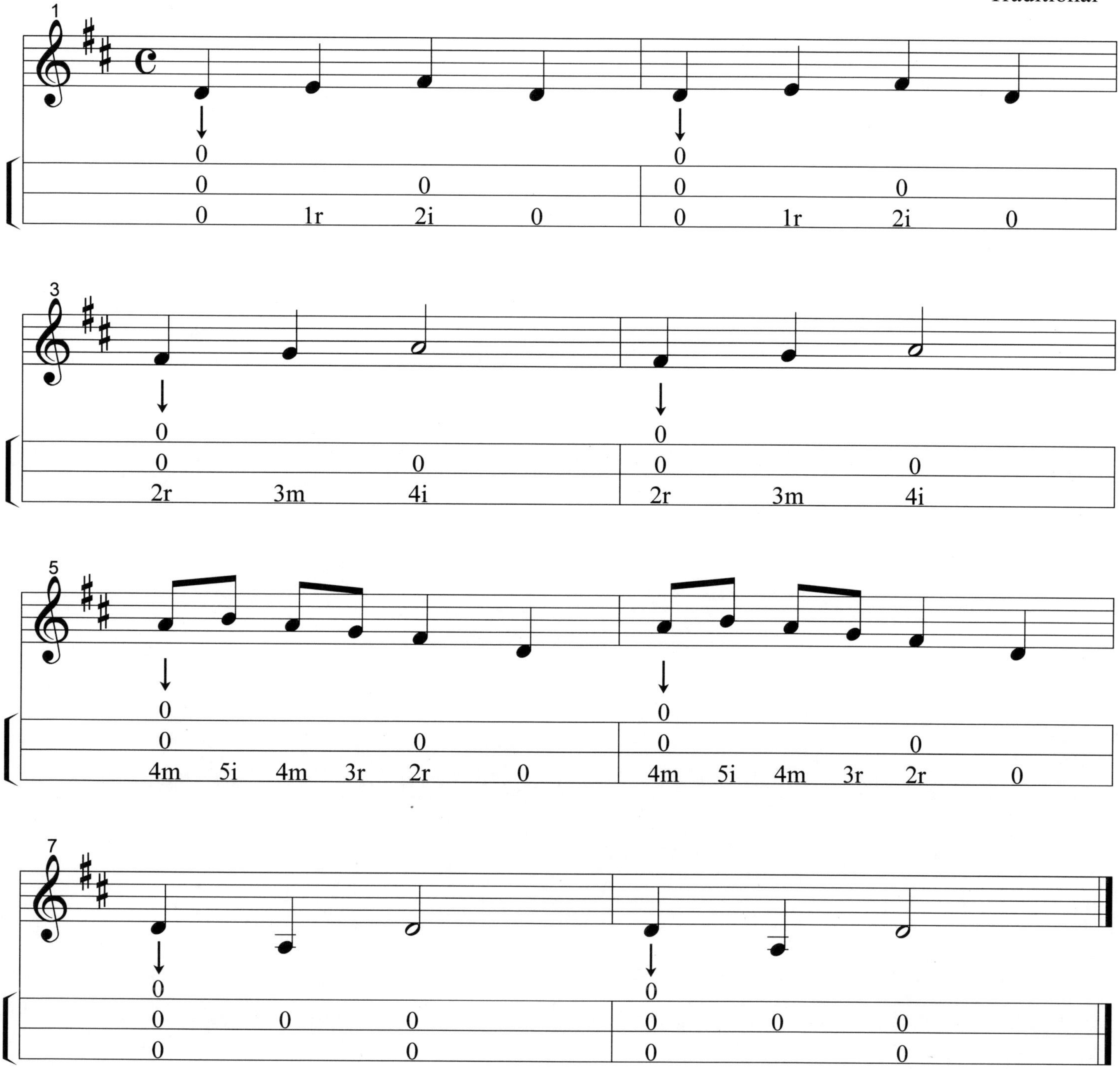

Next is a tune called "In the Air." Do just what you did with "Frère Jacques": strum with the arrows, pick the single notes and pluck everything else. Notice that it's in 3/4 time. Take a second to count out the timing – especially the first measure.

In the Air

©2015 Anne Dodson

DAD
1-5-8

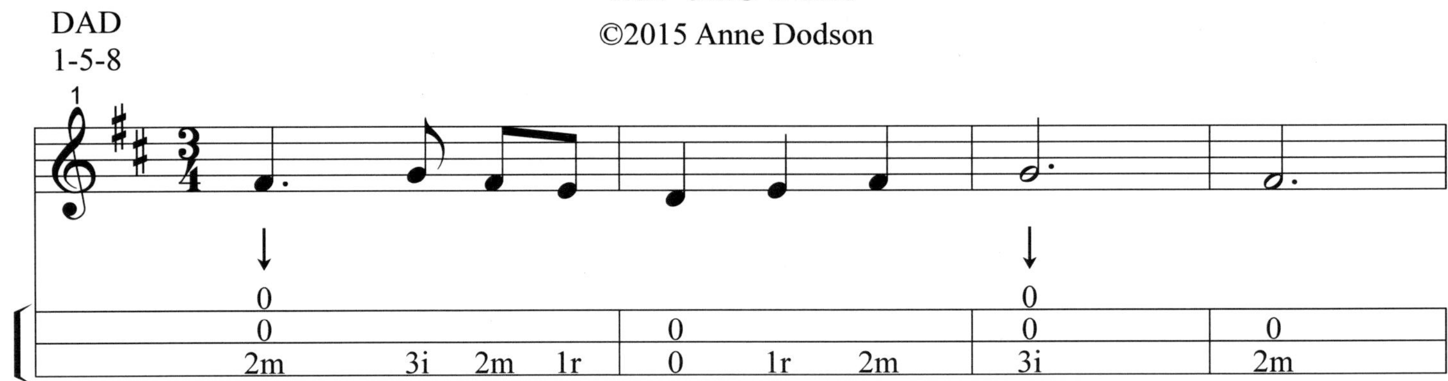

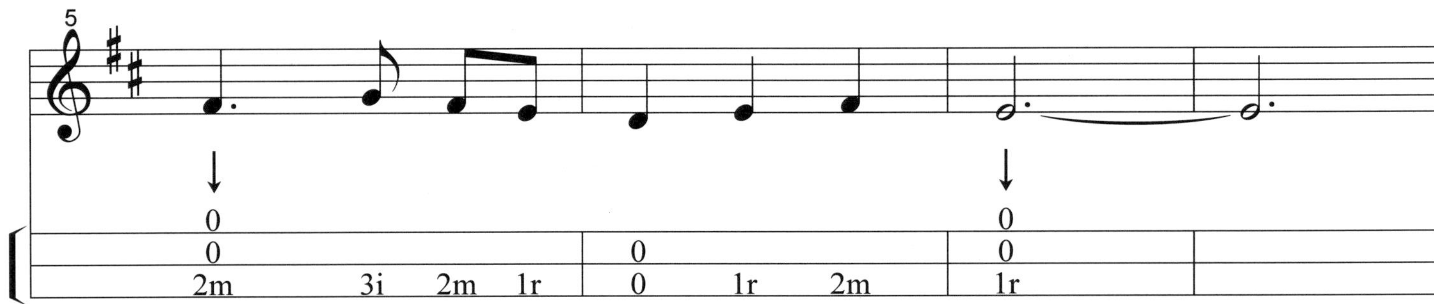

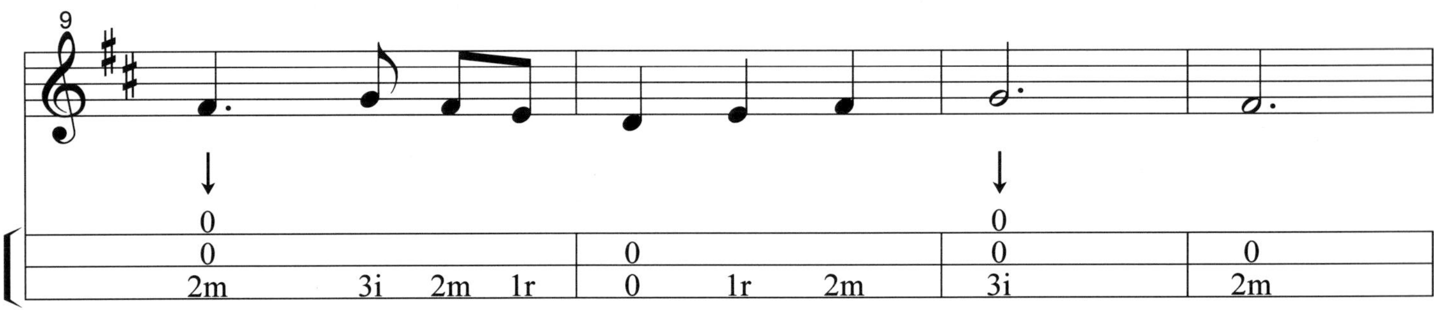

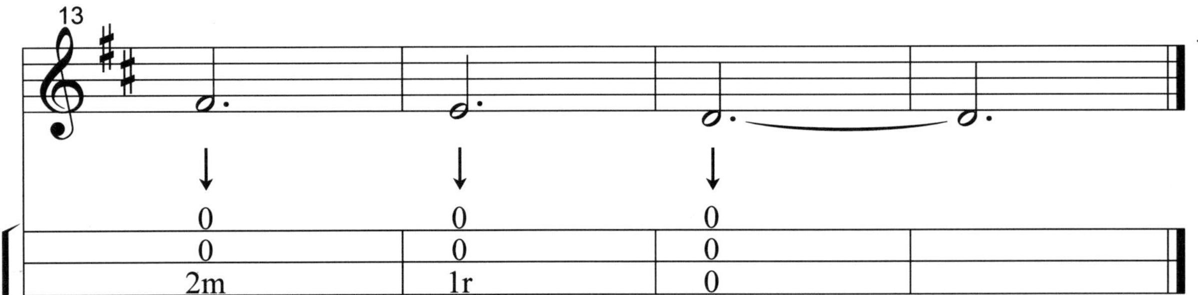

With the hard work you've done with your right hand you'll be able to move on to the next chapters with confidence. Don't worry if your brain and your hands are still not totally in sync. You'll be reinforcing the skills you've just learned in upcoming chapters. And you can always come back and rework areas that give you consistent problems.

Next up, we let your left hand run amok on all three strings!

Chapter 4 ~ Playing on All Three Strings

So far you've been using your left hand only on the first string of your dulcimer. Here's where you get to add fingering work on your middle and bass strings.

When you look at TAB that uses all three strings, you do exactly the same thing that you were doing on the first string – it's just that now there are fingering instructions on the other TAB lines as well. Sometimes it takes some real concentration to translate the TAB to your fingers, but trust me – it becomes easier and easier and even automatic after a while.

But, to start, you may have to think this through one step at a time. Take your time and pay attention to the fingering suggestions. If you get confused, back up a step and read the directions out loud.

Four-string equidistant players – from bass to treble, your lowest string is "bass," your third string is "middle," and the string closest to you is "first." Your second string just floats there as either a patient observer when picking or plucking, or a happy drone when strumming. You don't fret it with your left hand at all at this point. Its time will come!

First, let's get your bass string going. Recall "First Things #1." Here it is again, except this time you're playing the exercise on the bass string – the one farthest away from you. It's an octave lower than when you played it on your first string.

Track 28

Although the tune will sound different (since you're starting on an A note instead of a D note), you can play the same fingering on your middle string.

Track 29

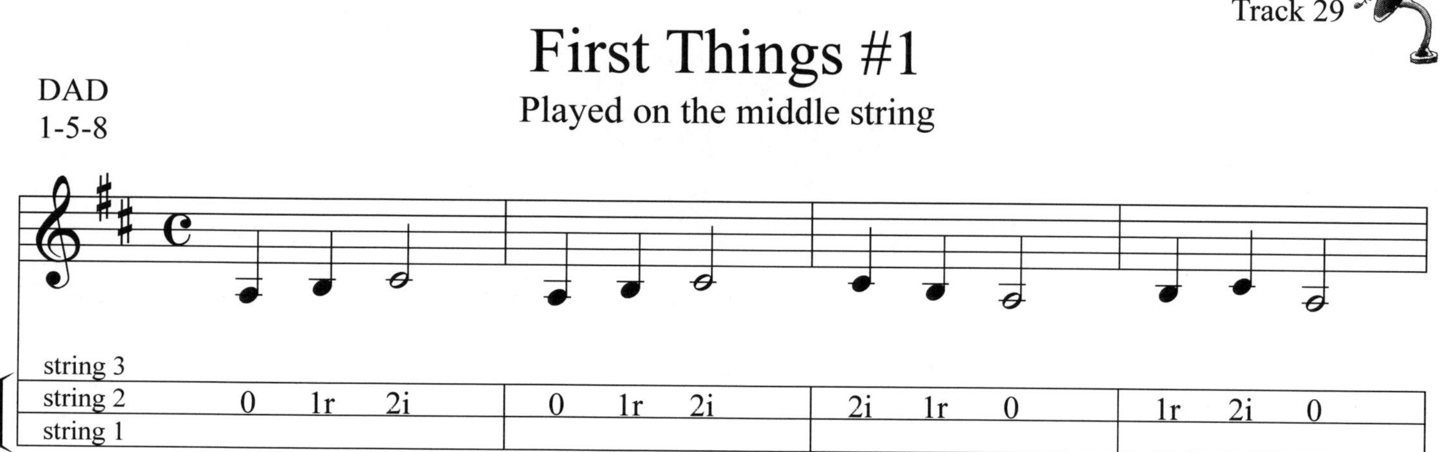

Let's get radical. Try this – watch the fingering.

More Strings #1

Here's the same tune, but this time you're playing in 3/4 time, so you'll have a little less time to make the transitions from one measure to the next. Take it as slowly as you need to so that you keep it in 3/4 and don't revert to 4/4.

More Strings #2

Staying in 3/4 time, try this next one. If you're having trouble, clap out the beats in 3/4 time before you start playing, keeping it slow and only building speed when you can play it smoothly.

Track 32

More Strings #3

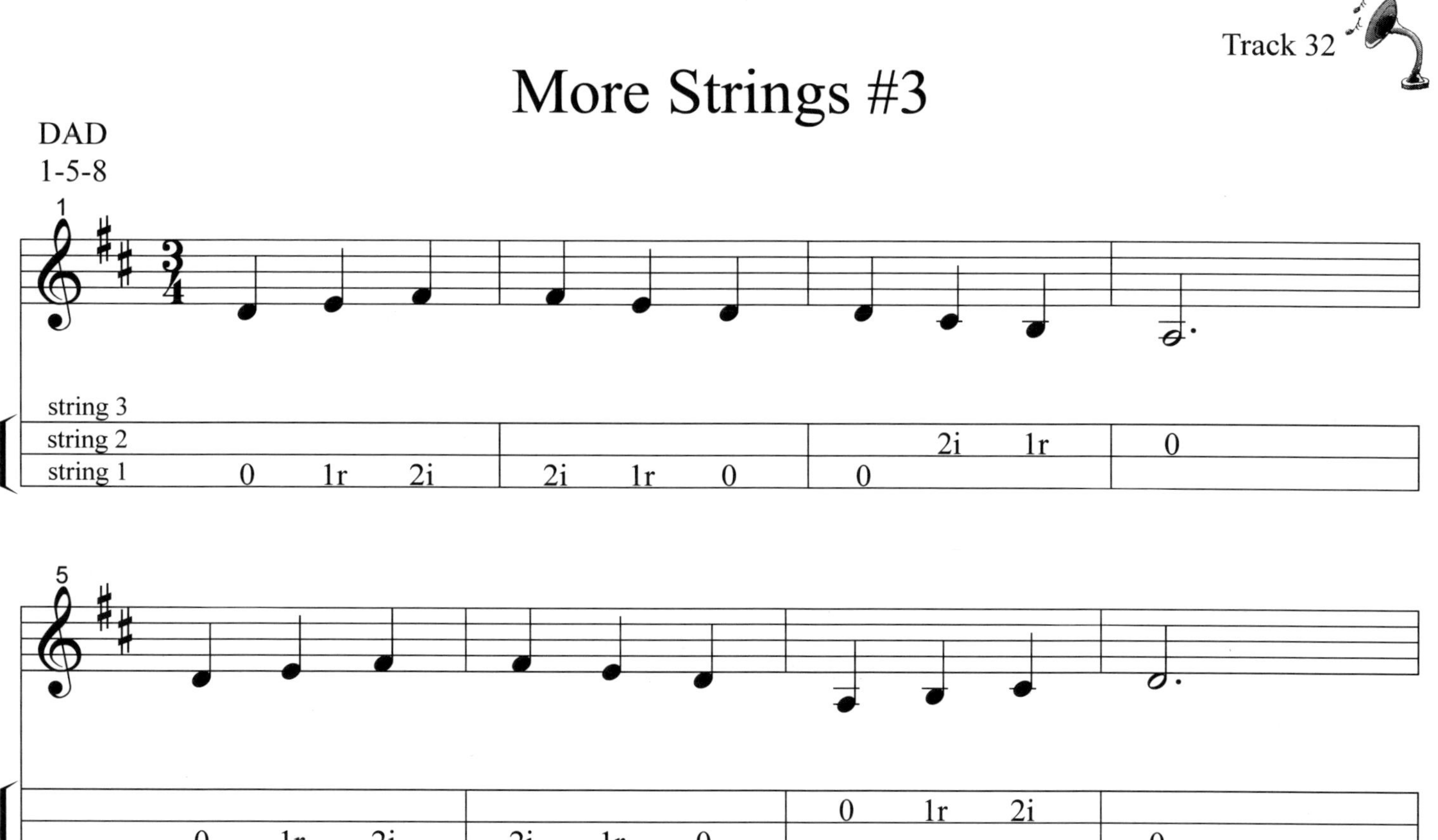

Is it starting to feel natural to move between the strings with your left hand? Are you keeping an eye on your right hand fingering? Remember to use your right hand thumb for your first string, your index finger for your middle string, and either your middle or index finger on the bass.

Now we switch back to 4/4 time:

More Strings #4

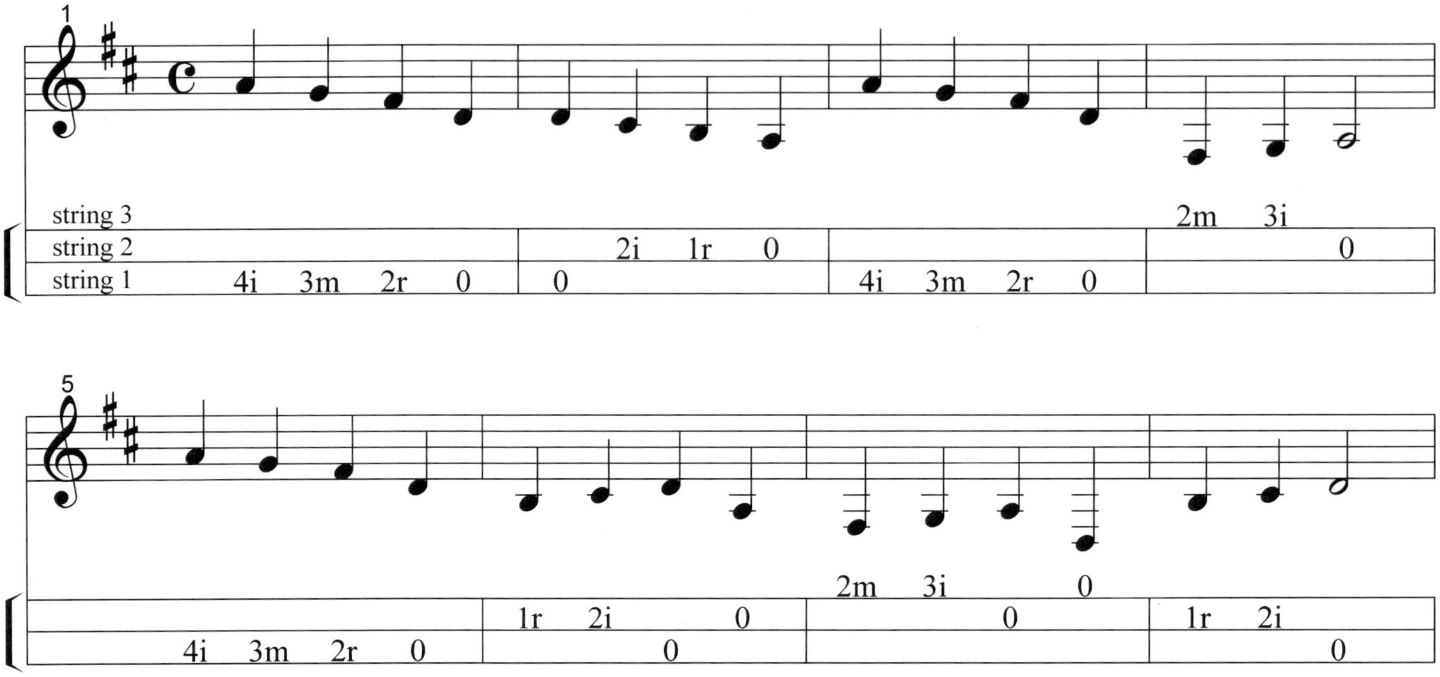

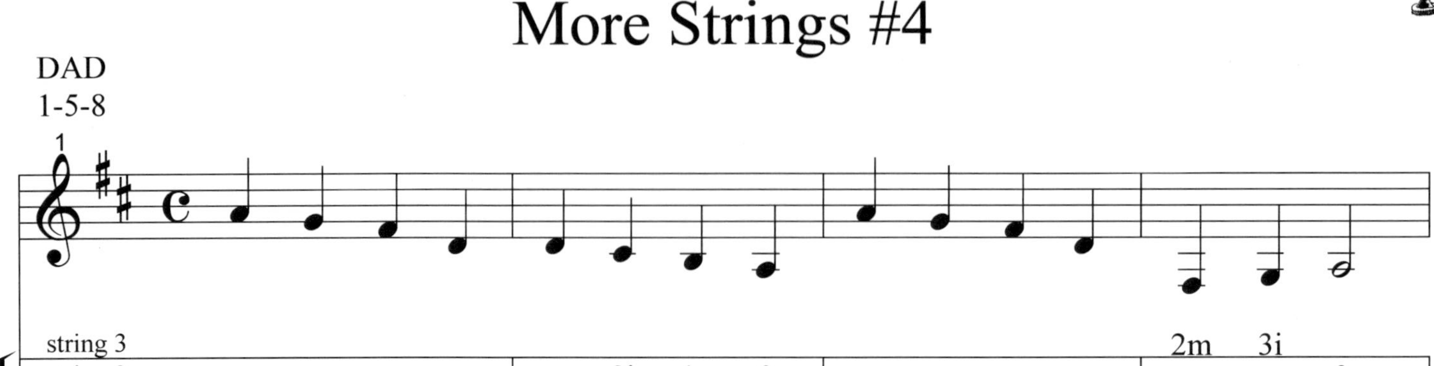

"More Strings #5" just moves around a little more. It's also a modified version of an old tune called "I Got a Gal at the Head of the Holler."

More Strings #5

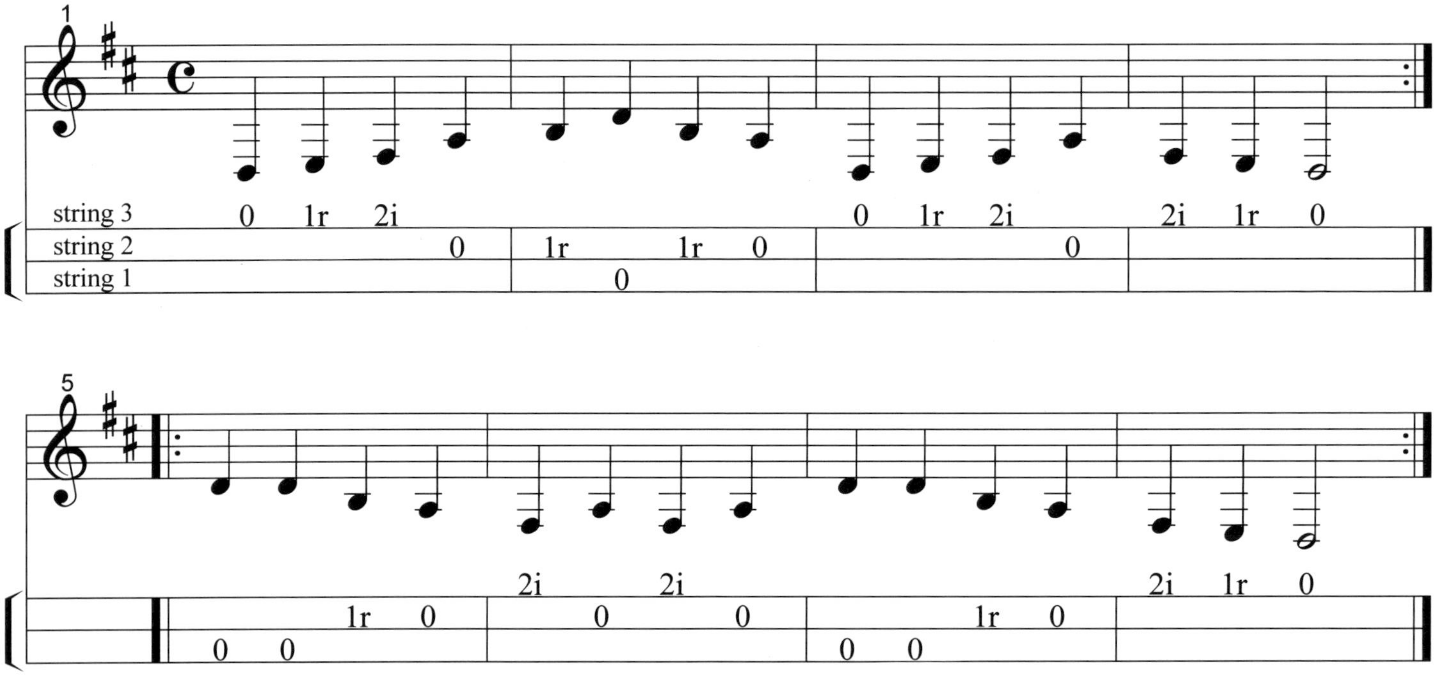

My friend Asha and I wrote "June Bug," thus named because it creeps and crawls around the fretboard. Play the first measure a few times – the melody doesn't go where you might expect. If you get overwhelmed by any part of this tune, try isolating two-measure sections and then piecing all the parts together. Have fun.[1]

Track 35

June Bug

©2015 Anne E. Dodson/Asha Stager

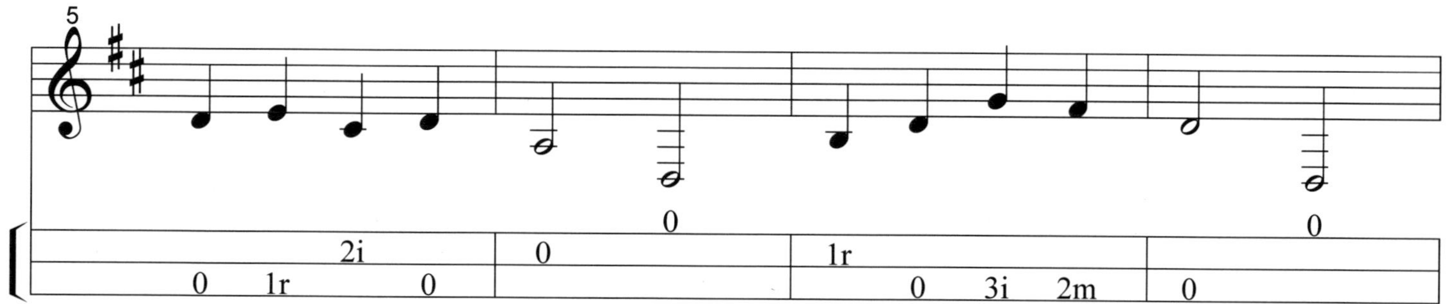

---

[1] If you're playing with a friend and you're feeling ambitious, "June Bug" is fun to play as a round.

Next up you get to combine what you've just been working on with some of the right hand techniques you learned in the last chapter. "Alabama Baby" is an exercise to prepare you for a wonderful old tune called "Alabama Gal."

Alabama Baby

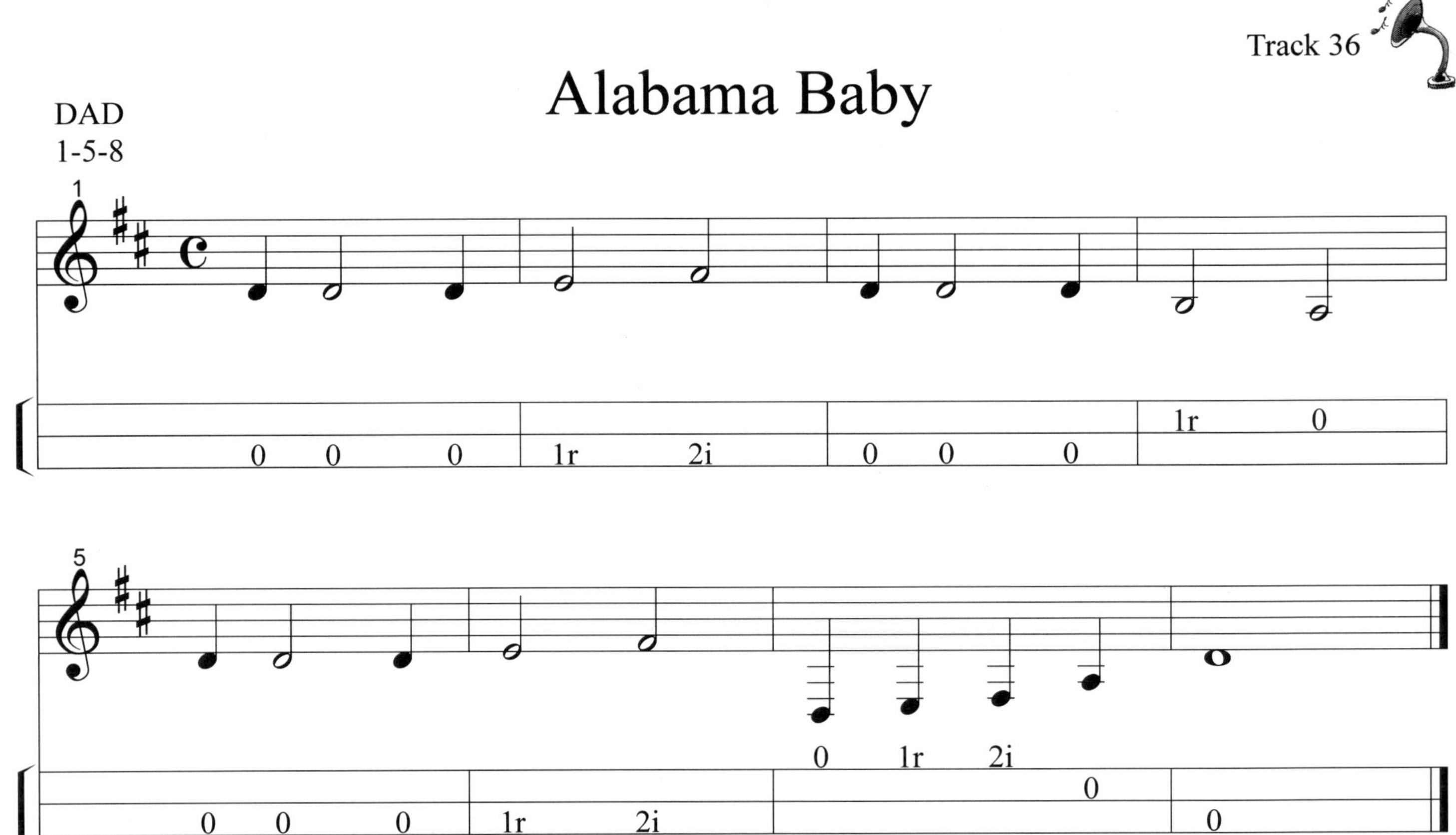

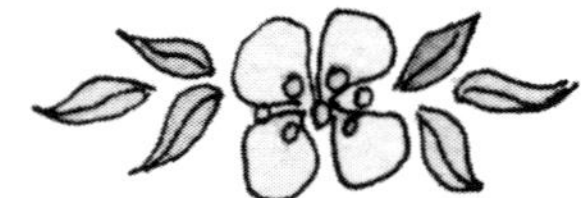

Now you're ready to move on to "Alabama Gal." You're venturing onto the middle string only twice in this tune, but you're also incorporating right hand strumming. Watch the direction of the arrows – there are places where you'll be strumming "away" twice in a row. When you finger the middle string, continue to strum straight across – you'll be tempted to pick the note singly.

When you play measures #10, #12 and #14, you may curse me a bit. Think of it as Alzheimer's prevention. It will also help to realize that the strumming pattern for this piece is to always strum "away" on the first beat of each measure.

I strongly suggest that you play it through a time or two with just your right hand playing the rhythm – don't get your left hand involved until you have a handle on the timing. Pay close attention to whether you're playing a whole note, half note, quarter or eighth, and give each note its due. Add the left hand fingering when you feel ready. This might be a good time to bring out that flat pick, or you could just use your index finger.

Alabama Gal

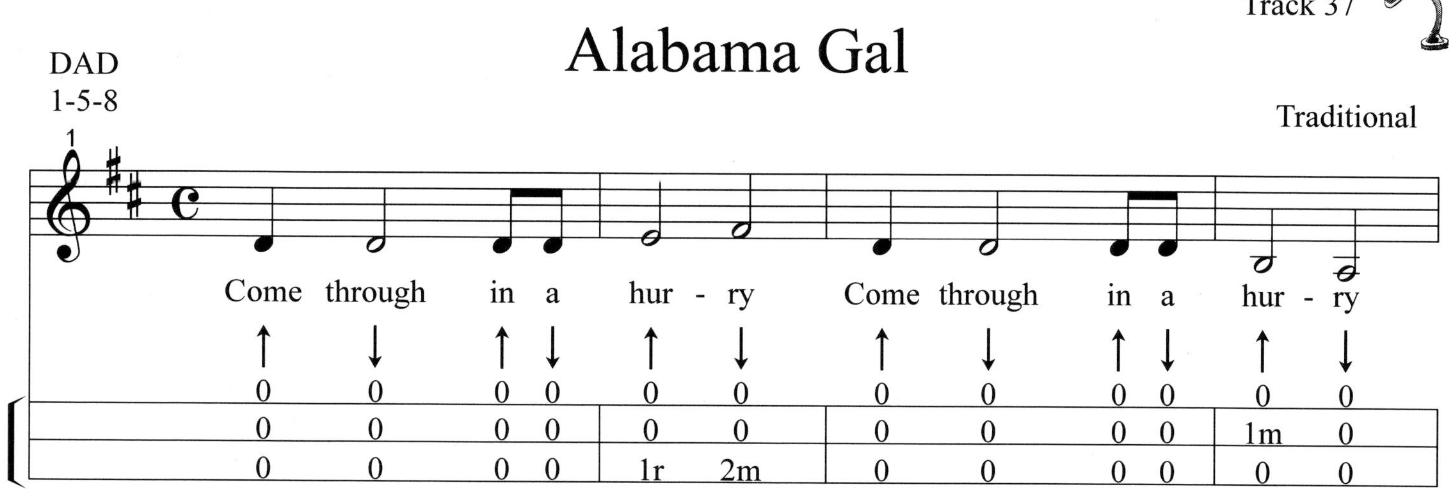

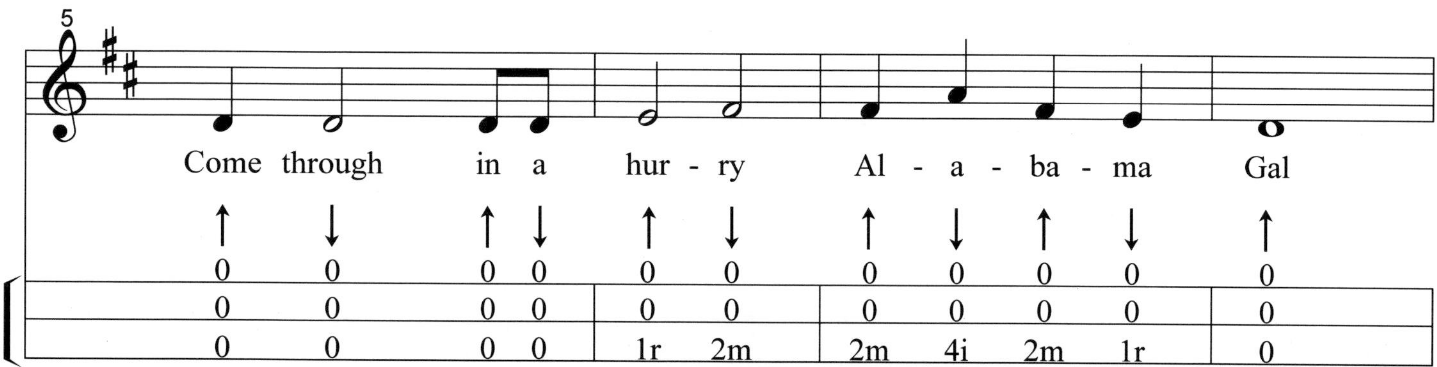

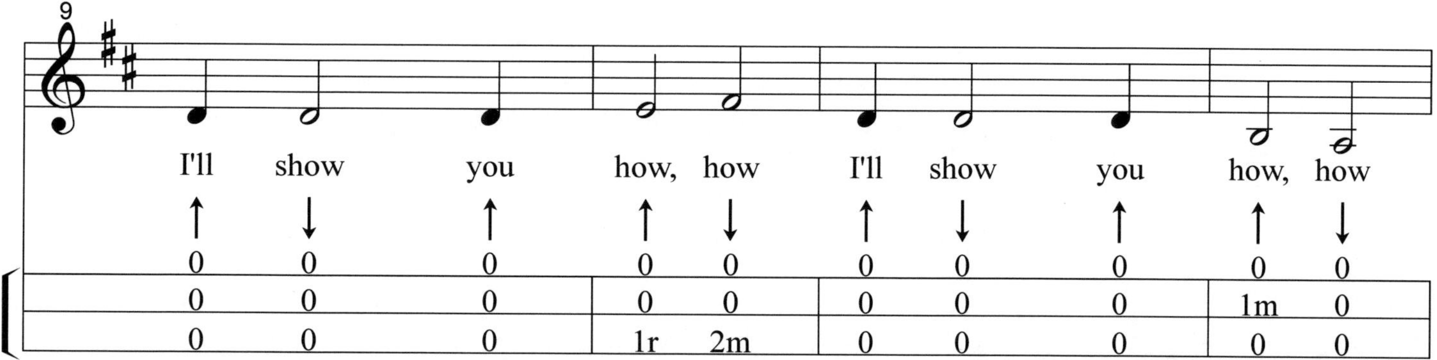

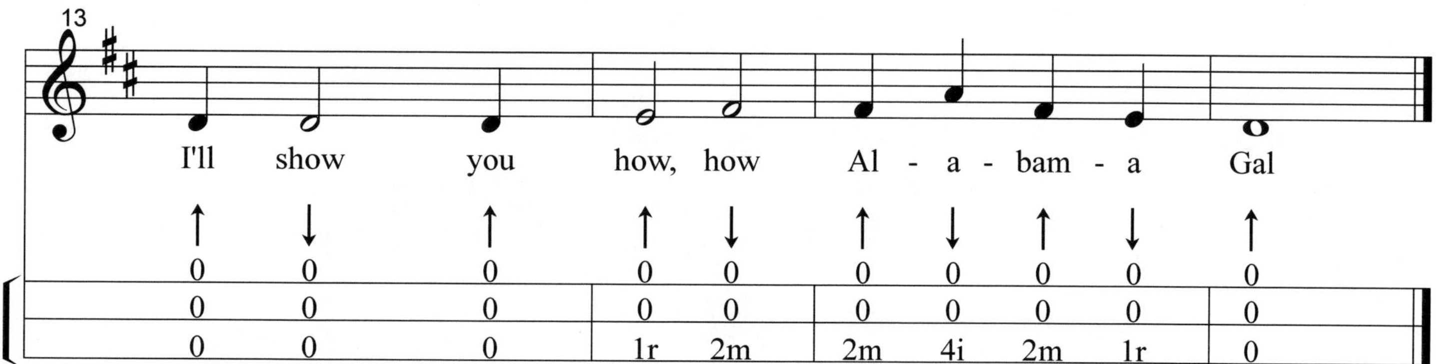

And, once you've got the control, there's no reason not to experiment with strumming it your own way if it feels as if you'd naturally do it differently. I tried "Alabama Gal" a number of ways before I settled on the pattern I indicated. It could have gone in a number of different directions.

As we move to the end of this chapter, I want to give you a little bridge into the next chapter, which is all about chords. If you don't know technically what a chord is, hang on – that's coming up. What you're going to be doing is placing more than one finger at a time on different strings on the fretboard instead of putting left hand fingers down sequentially.

Remember the fingerpicking and strumming that we did in the last chapter? In the following exercises, you'll encounter familiar patterns with your right hand, but now you get to add a little more with your left hand.
- In this first one, place your ring finger on the 2nd fret of your first string and keep it there.
- Then, take your index finger and place it on the 3rd fret on your middle string (keep your middle finger out of the picture for now!).
- Hold both of those strings down – hey! You're playing a chord.
- You can strum in either direction or pluck all three notes with your right hand.

Track 38

Strumming (or plucking) #5

DAD
1-5-8

It'll get easier and is, in fact, the foundation to a lot of what you'll be doing in the rest of this book. So, spend some more time with it. Strum it, pluck it, get comfortable with it.

So… you're ready to tackle the next exercise. Look over "Fingerpicking #12." Notice that your left hand is playing the same "form" that you just played, but your right hand gets to do a little more.

- Pick that open bass string with either the middle or index finger of your right hand.
- Then, pluck your middle and first strings with your index and thumb. You did this same pattern with "Fingerpicking #4" and "Fingerpicking #10" in the last chapter. Go back and review those two exercises if you think it would be helpful.

Track 39

Fingerpicking #12

Next up, same thing except for one small change with your right hand.

- This time you pick your bass string and then *strum* the chord (toward you, eh?) with your index finger.
- Pick your bass string again and then *pluck* your first and middle strings. If you need a reminder, it's the same pattern as "Fingerpicking #9 and #11" in the last chapter.

Track 40

Fingerpicking #13

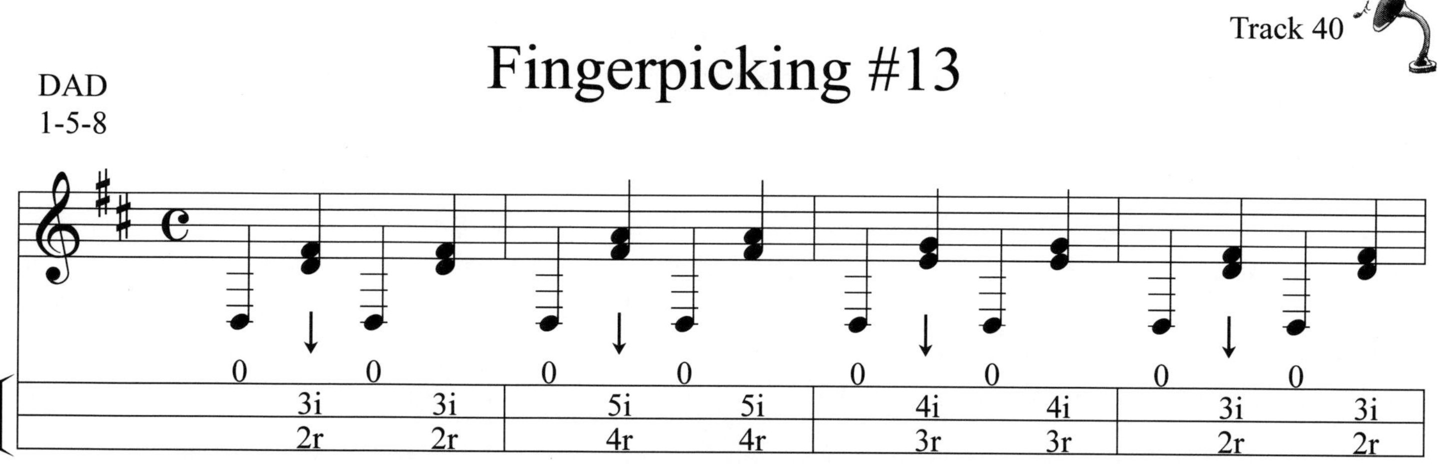

I know – it can make your brain hurt. But you've done it! Congratulate yourself and then take a deep breath. I say you're ready to move on to chords.

Chapter 5 ~ Chords and How They Work on the Dulcimer

A chord is most often defined as three or more different notes played together. If you don't know basic music theory you may need to take parts of this chapter on faith and fill in some of the blanks later on. We'll expand on the theory behind chords at the beginning of Book 2, with a chapter entitled "Basic Chord Structure."

In this chapter we will explore:
- The three most important chords in the key of D.
- Different ways to play those three chords.
- More chords, including some minor chords.
- "Undefined" chords (or "how to cheat on the dulcimer and get away with it").
- The difference between major and minor chords.
- How to recognize the chords you're playing.
- The importance of memorizing selected chords (some polite nagging involved).

First position chords

When we refer to "positions," we're simply talking about where the chords are played on the fretboard. First position chords are played within the first 3 or 4 frets. Second position chords are played higher up the fretboard.

There are usually a number of different ways to play any given chord on your instrument. Since in DAD/DADD tuning we're tuned to a D chord, there are tons of ways to play a D chord (more so than other chords). You'll find many of those in the general chord chart later on in this chapter. But what we're going to start with are the simplest ways to play a D chord, a G chord and an A chord. These three chords will make sense to your "western" ears when you hear them played together. You'll hear all three played in track 41.

First up is the First Position D chord. You've already played it in some of the fingerpicking exercises.
- Place the ring finger of your left hand on the first string, 2nd fret.
- Strum straight across. Voilá! You've played a D chord.

Track 41 

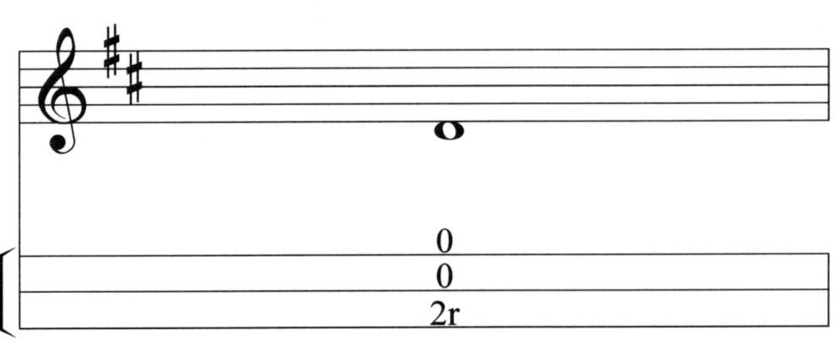

Now move on to the first position G chord. If your mind balks, it might help if you talk it through out loud:

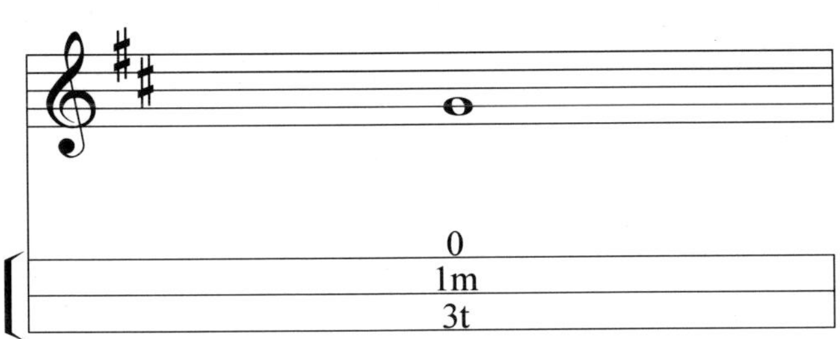

- Your bass string is open (0).
- Place your middle finger on the 1st fret of your middle string (1m) *(third string for you four-stringers)*.
- Place your thumb on the 3rd fret of your first string (3t).
- Strum.

Nice, right? Do the same thing for the first position A chord. (*Four-string equidistant players: you may notice some dissonance with this chord when you let your second string ring out open. That's because you're "lingering" on the chord. It'll sound better when you hear it in context. Let it go for now.*) Talk this one through out loud as well:

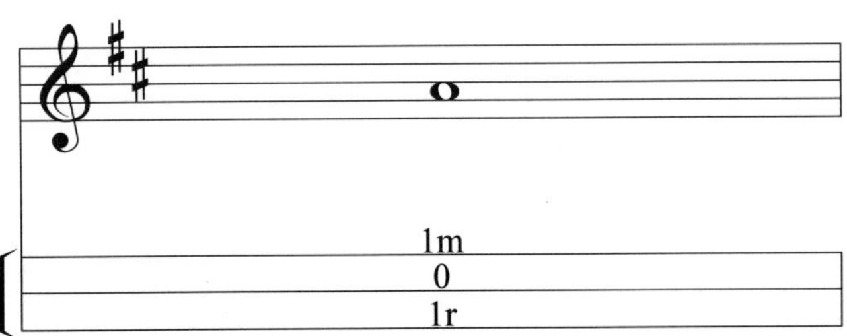

- Place your middle finger on the 1st fret of your bass string (1m).
- Leave your middle string, open (0).
- Place your ring finger on the 1st fret of your first string (1r).
- Strum.

Here are the same first position chords, played in progression:

Track 42

First Position DGA Progression

DAD
1-5-8

D	G	A	D
0	0	1m	0
0	1m	0	0
2r	3t	1r	2r

D	A	G	D
0	1m	0	0
0	0	1m	0
2r	1r	3t	2r

Play around with "First Position DGA Progression" as it's written. Then try playing the three chords in a different order, getting familiar with moving from one to the next. In all likelihood, your ears will decide to start with and resolve to the D chord. That's because it's "home base" (or the "root") in the key of D.

Those three chords sound "right," right? With just those three chords you can play a ton of songs. Many, many songs, including plenty of simple folk songs, use only three chords.

Here's a version of "Simple Gifts," using the first position chords that you just learned. The melody is written in the upper staff, but the TAB shows the chords that you'd play if you were singing the song or accompanying an instrumentalist. Important thing to recognize: you are not playing the melody of the song in this instance. You're playing an accompaniment to your singing.

Notice how the chord name is written up over the staff. You'll see this frequently used in this and other books. To find the first note for singing "Simple Gifts" in this key, play your open A string.

Simple Gifts

First position chords

Joseph Brackett 1848

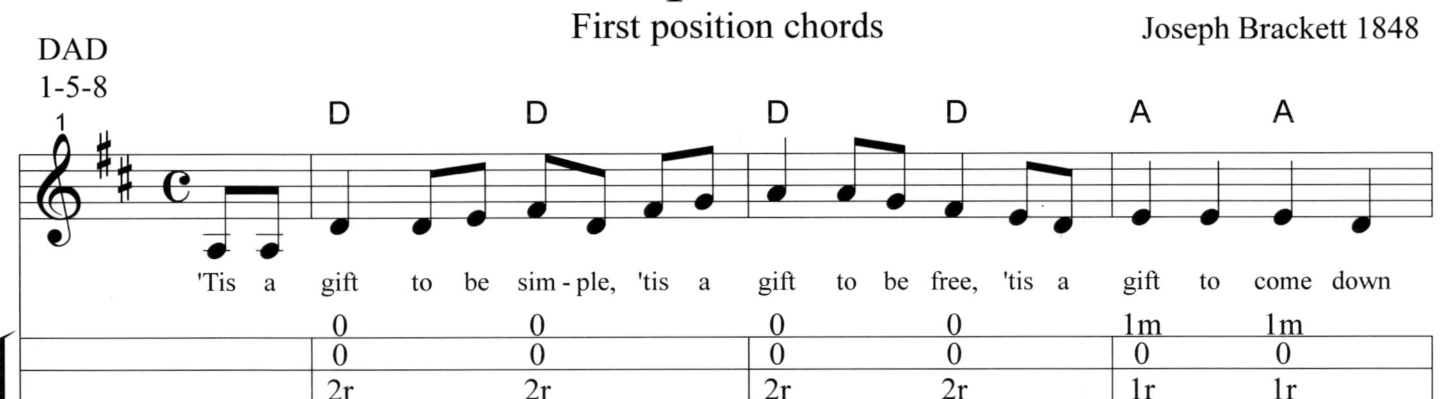

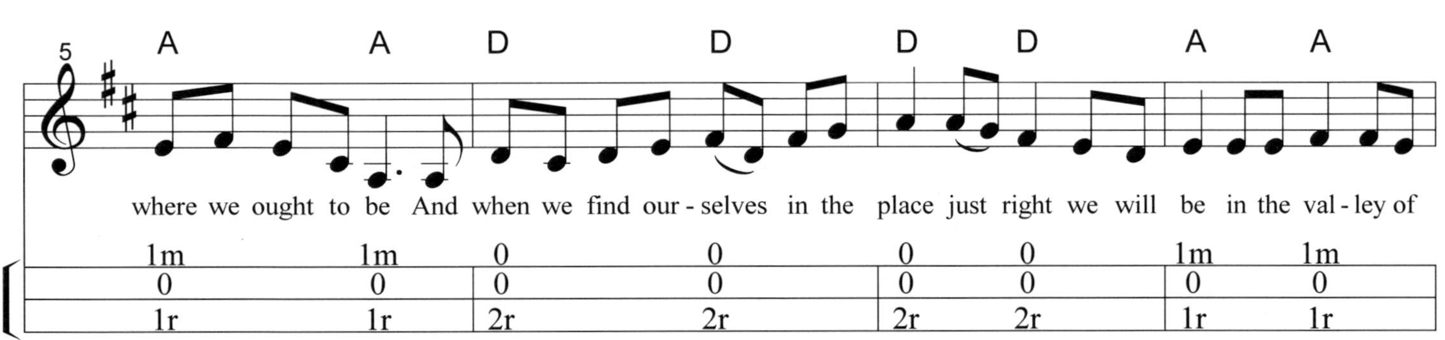

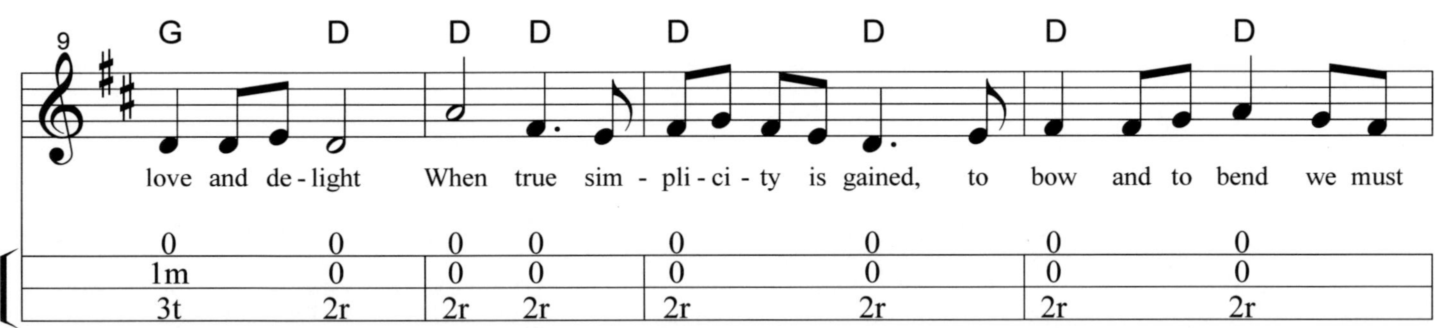

Here's another song with which you can practice those first position chords. Play it with "bum-did-dees" if you feel like it, or you can just strum if you need a break.

Oh Susannah

First postition chords

Stephen Foster 1848

DAD
1-5-8

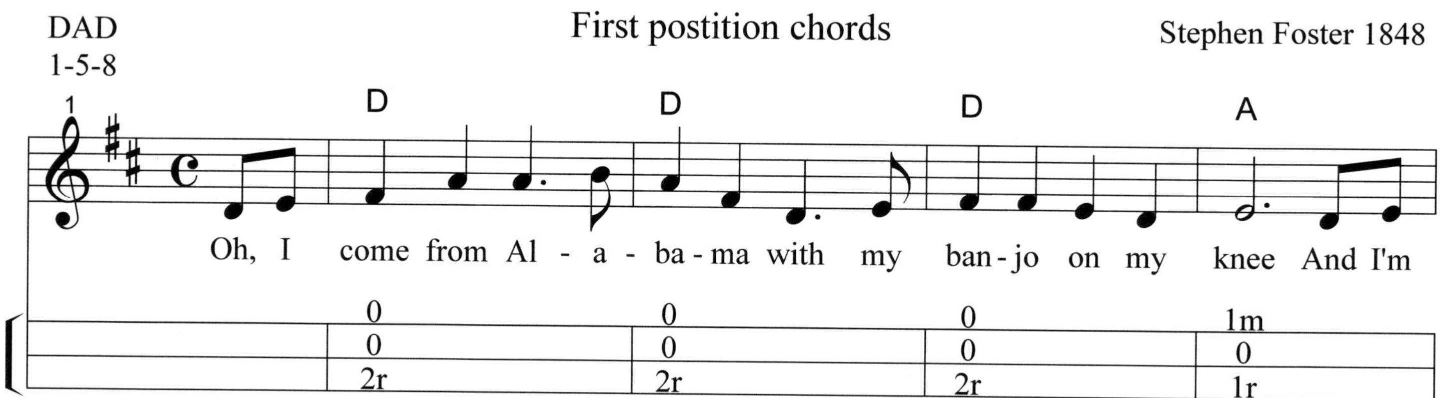

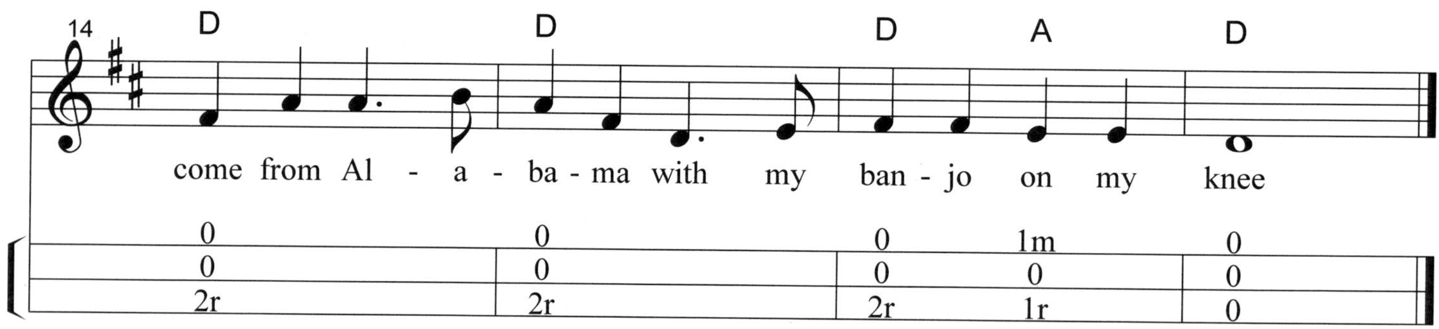

Here's an assignment for you. See if you can discover the first position chords you'd play to accompany "She'll Be Comin' Round the Mountain." Fill in the chord names in the boxes above the staff and then write in the TAB in the open TAB lines below; we'll revisit this worksheet, so you may want to make a photocopy. The first one is done for you (suggested answers are on the next page). Here are some hints:

- A majority of songs start and end in their "home" key… in this case, it's the key of D.
- Play a chord as you sing the song – if it sounds right, it *is* right.
- Keep playing that chord until it clashes with the melody.
- Choose another chord – does it sound correct? Keep it. If not, try another.
- Your palette for this song only includes the chords D, G and A!

Give yourself some time to work it out before you look ahead for my suggestions.

She'll Be Comin' Round the Mountain

DAD
1-5-8

Traditional

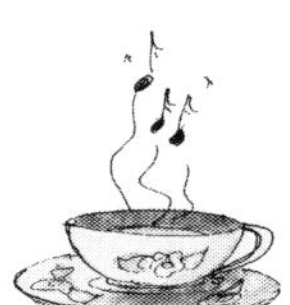

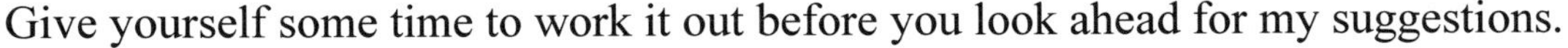

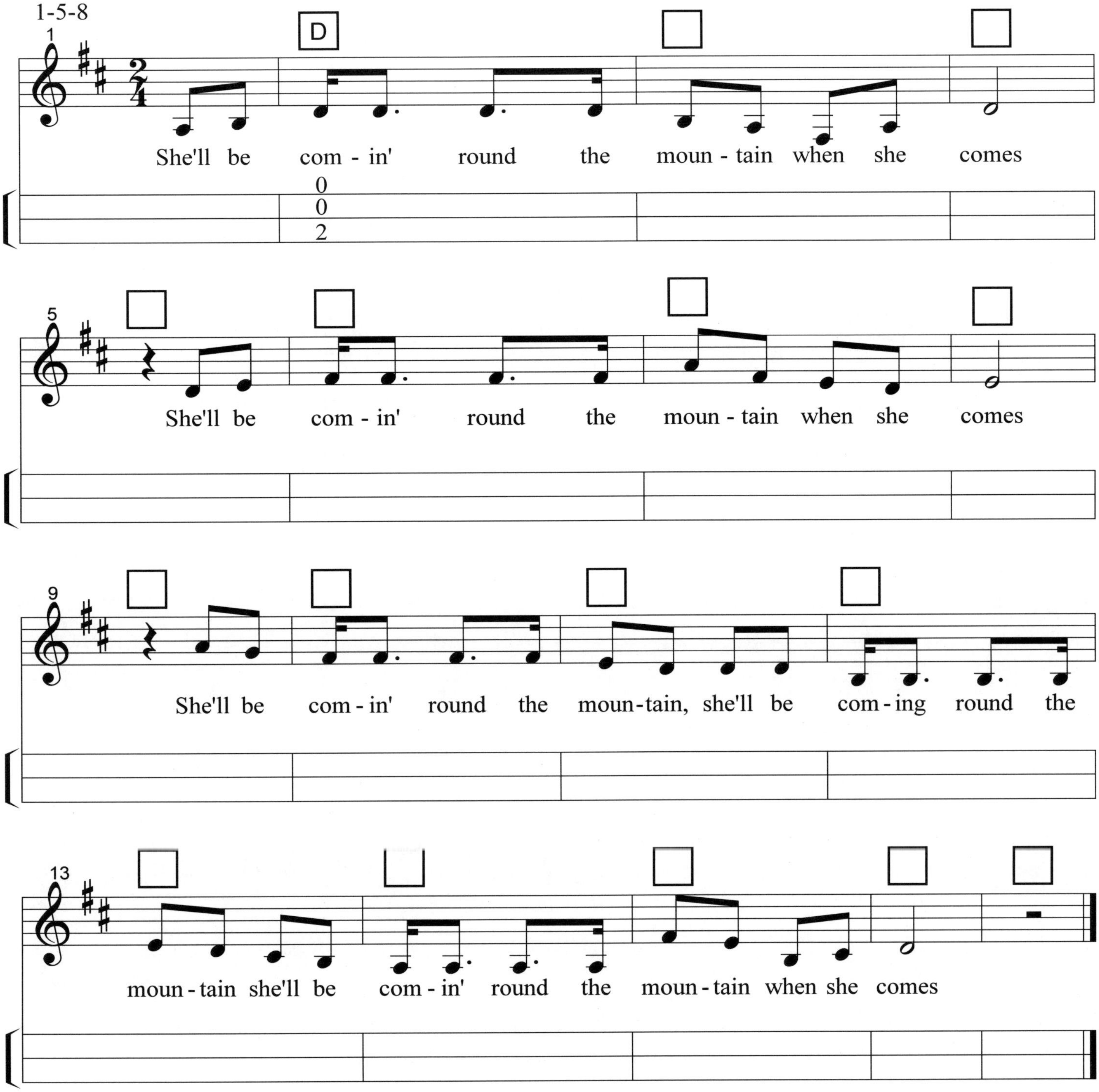

How did it go? This is what I would suggest…

She'll Be Comin' Round the Mountain

Traditional

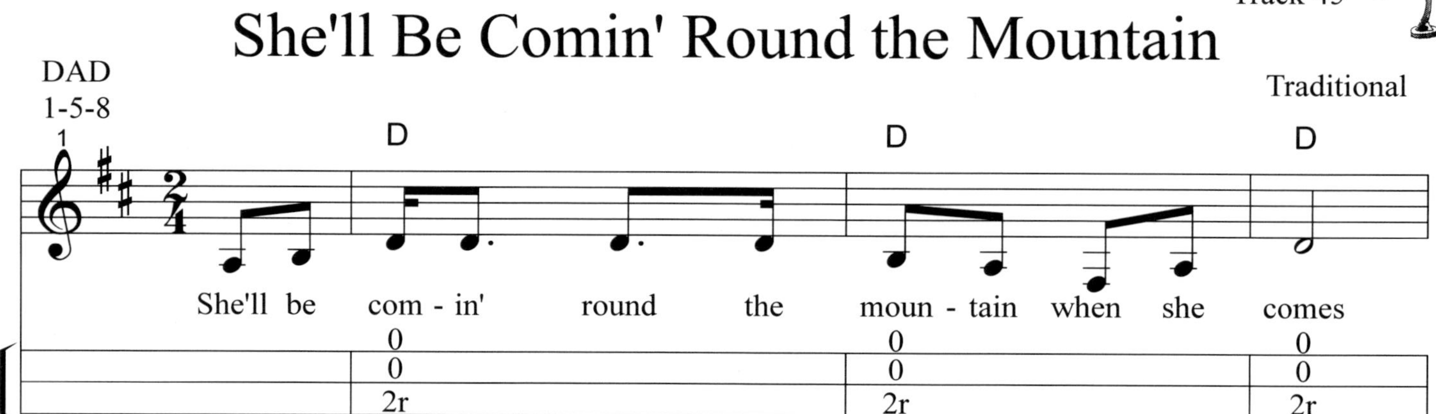

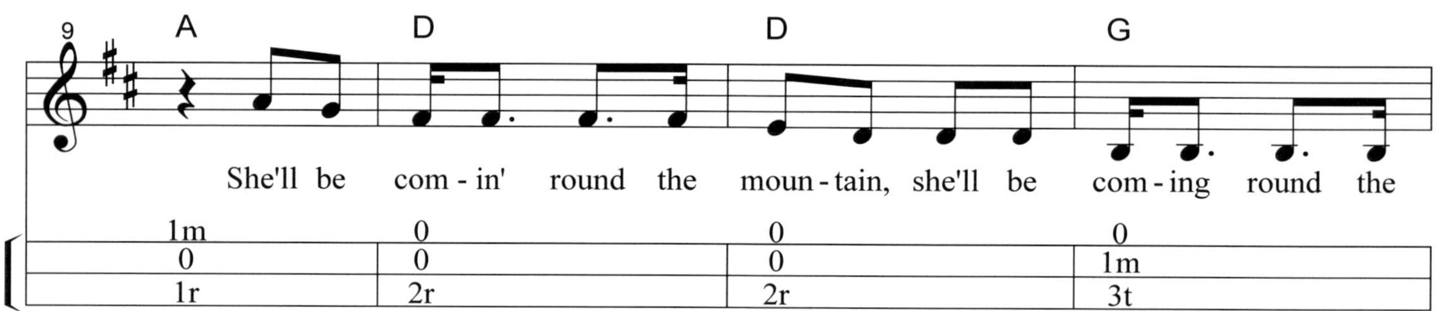

Looking for even more of a challenge? Something like *Rise Up Singing*, which is a book of lyrics and chords to well-known songs, would be a good resource for finding other songs to play. Look for songs that start and end with a D chord and use D, G and A as their only chords. You might also find that just by playing these chords, ideas for other songs come to mind.

You'll notice that I call these three chords that you just learned, played within the first three frets, "first position chords." You might not find other teachers/players using that same term, but if you pointed it out to them, I suspect they would say, "Oh, yeah – that makes sense." It's the same term that is used for playing chords on the guitar that are close to the headstock.

You've played "In The Air" before. Here it is again, but this time you'll be adding first position chords to enhance the melody. You'll also be incorporating some of the right hand techniques that you learned in the chapter about fingerpicking. Watch the left hand fingering suggestions (there are minor differences from what you played before) but if you find that your left hand naturally fingers it differently than I play it, remember that it's fine to go with whatever feels best to you; just aim for consistency.

If you get overwhelmed, simplify the process (try just strumming and not plucking, for instance). But attempt the whole thing first and see how it goes. This time you *are* playing the melody of the tune *and* you're framing that melody with chords as well!

Track 46

In the Air

©2015 Anne Dodson

Here are two more chords that I consider to be first position chords. They are alternate ways of playing a D chord and an A chord:

The D chord (0,3,2) has a nice warm, full sound and the A (1,2,4) is more balanced than the A you've been using (1,0,1). However, they are both a bit more challenging to play. If your hands and brain are feeling ready, you can go back and try them out with "Oh Susannah" and "Simple Gifts."

Second position chords

The next exercise will show you how to play what is often my favorite way of playing D/G/A chords. All three chords are close together on the fretboard, as they were in the last section, but this time you'll be playing them in a different place. You'll hear that they are the same chords you played before in the sense that each chord is composed of the same three notes, but in a different order or octave. I think of it as the same chord but with a different "coloring."

When you try "Second Position Chords," make sure that you've got the fingering right. There are reasons why I finger these chords this way that might not be obvious at this point, but you'll be glad you put in the time now when we start working more with these chords later on. Notice that the G chord and the A chord use the same fingering – they are just on different frets. So, to move from the G to the A all you have to do is slide the whole "form" up the fretboard. Same thing coming down from the A to the G – just slide the whole thing down without changing your left hand finger position. We'll be dealing with this concept more in Book 2, in the chapter about chord forms. Try this:

Second Position Chords

DAD
1-5-8

D	D	G	D
0	0	3m	0
5i	5i	3r	5i
4r	4r	5t	4r

G	A	D	A
3m	4m	0	4m
3r	4r	5i	4r
5t	6½t	4r	6½t

D	D	G	D
0	0	3m	0
5i	5i	3r	5i
4r	4r	5t	4r

G	A	G	D
3m	4m	3m	0
3r	4r	3r	5i
5t	6½t	5t	4r

If finding the fingering was difficult, you might cultivate the habit of talking through, out loud, what finger belongs on which fret, as we did for the first position chords. Now play "Simple Gifts" and "Oh Susannah" using these new positions.

Simple Gifts

Second position chords

Joseph Brackett 1848

Oh Susannah

Second postition chords

Stephen Foster 1848

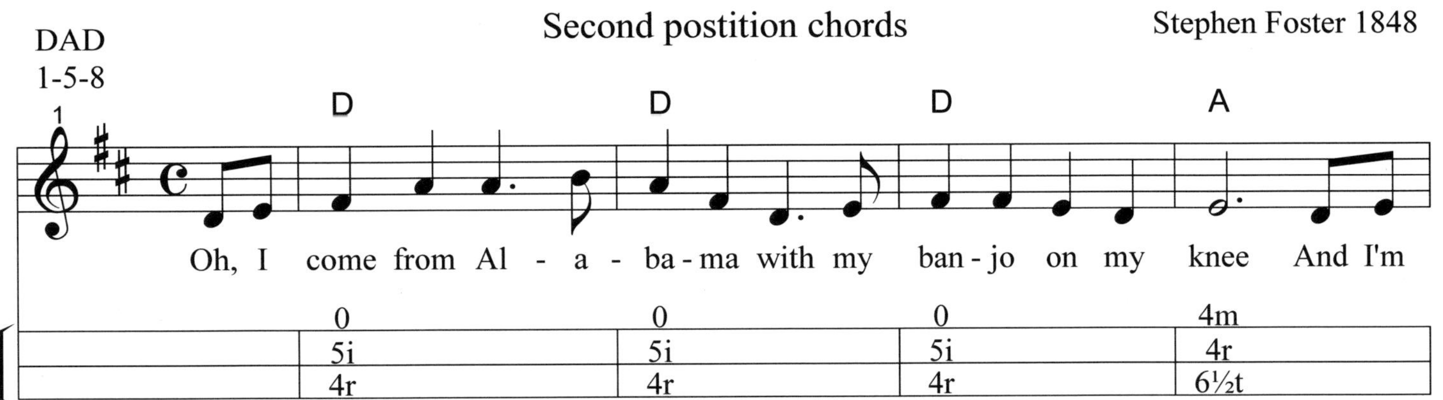

Fun, eh? (Don't give me that look!) For any song, when you get comfortable with one version of the chords, challenge yourself by playing the chords in a different position. How about an extra credit assignment? Go back to your worksheet for "She'll Be Comin' Round the Mountain" (page 65) and substitute second position chords for the first position chords!

More chords

So you're getting the hang of playing D/G/A chords in two different places on the fretboard and you're learning how to move from one chord to the other. Now it's time to bring in some new chords. The next chart, "More Chords," will help you identify and play at least one fingering for all of the chords you'll need to play simple songs in the *keys* of D, G and A. You'll also have many of the chords you'll need for more complex songs. A small "m" after the chord name means it's a minor chord (Em = E minor).

Work your way through "More Chords." Your first chord is a D, played 0,0,2. Now move up to the Em chord. Pay attention to the left hand fingering. *(Remember, if you're playing a four-string equidistant instrument, let that second string stay open as a drone and finger the chord on strings one, three and four.)* Move your fingers, in that same position, up the fretboard to 2,2,4. That's an F♯m. Slide up one more, it becomes a G.

Slide it up one more fret. You'll notice that your thumb comes to rest on the 6th fret. That's an Am chord. You can form an A chord by moving just your *thumb* up to the 6½ fret. This is one of the many reasons I like the 6½ fret. It lets you form a nice full A chord. A nice full A chord is a very, very good thing.

Keep moving up the fretboard to find the Bm, C and then yet another way of making a nice, higher sounding D chord at 7,7,9.

If you're playing four-string equidistant, you may have noticed some spots that sounded dissonant. That's what I meant when I referred earlier to the depth that you get from having that extra string as a drone. If it doesn't sound right to you, remember that you're lingering on the chord as you're learning to play it, and, for the most part, you'll be moving more quickly as you become more conversant with the chords.

Although many of the chords create that dissonant "rubbing," the only one that seems to really bother some people is the A chord. If it gets to you, you can finger the four strings 4,4,4,6½, using your pinkie to fret the second string on the 4th fret. You could also alter your fingering so that you're using your index, middle and ring finger to play the three lower strings. This will get rid of the "bad" note, but to my ears that "bad" note brings back some of the traditional open sound to the instrument. If you can, be patient and let that second string ring. I suspect you'll begin to hear it as an advantage as it blends in.

Getting acquainted with minors

Next up, you use just two of the chords that we've been discussing: the D, which is fingered 0,0,2 and the Em chord, fingered 1,1,3. You'll be playing in a minor key for the first time.

In "Shady Grove" I like to play the D chord by fretting the 2nd fret with my thumb. Some of my students prefer to use their middle finger. Experiment and see what feels best to you. You're just playing accompaniment to your singing here. *For four-string equidistant players, "Shady Grove" may be an exception to the "let the second string ring through" concept. Since it's in the key of Em, instead of our usual D, I don't always love hearing that open D note in such a dominant position. I might, in fact, finger it 1,1,1,3, using my index, middle, ring fingers and thumb or my middle, ring, pinkie and thumb. It's your choice as to how many strings you want to cover and how you finger the chord. In the sound file, I left the second string open. And I expect you to be consistent – hmmmm.*

Shady Grove

Track 51

DAD
1-5-8
Traditional
Em D Em Em
Cheeks as red as a bloom-ing rose   Hair a chest-nut brown
1m 0 1m 1m
1r 0 1r 1r
3t 2t 3t 3t

Em D Em D Em
Eyes the co-lor of the sky be - fore the rain comes down
1m 0 1m 0 1m
1r 0 1r 0 1r
3t 2t 3t 2t 3t

Em D Em Em
Sha - dy Grove, my true love   Sha - dy Grove my dar - lin'
1m 0 1m 1m
1r 0 1r 1r
3t 2t 3t 3t

Em D Em D Em
Sha - dy Grove, my true love   I'm go-in' back to Har - lan
1m 0 1m 0 1m
1r 0 1r 0 1r
3t 2t 3t 2t 3t

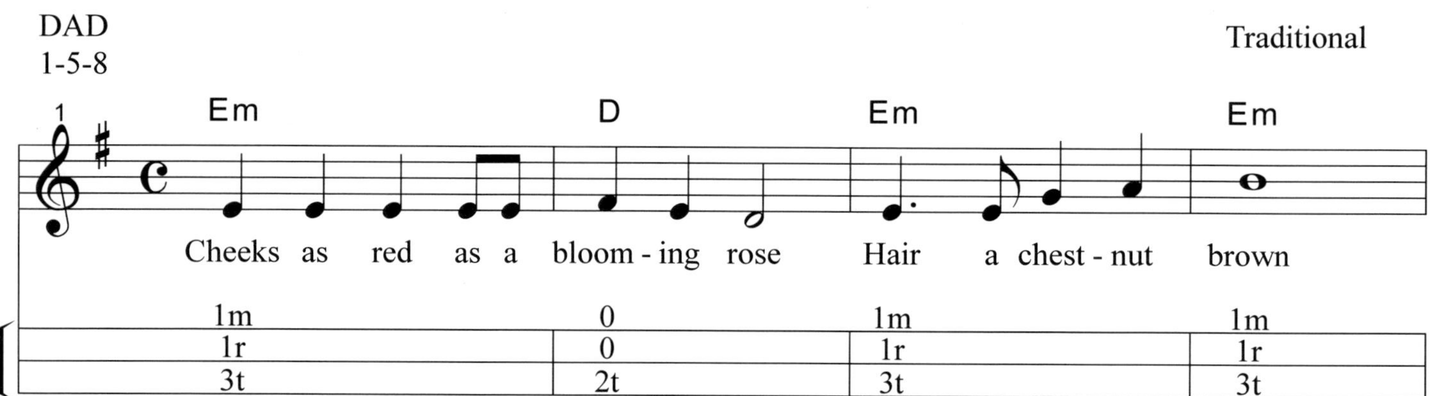

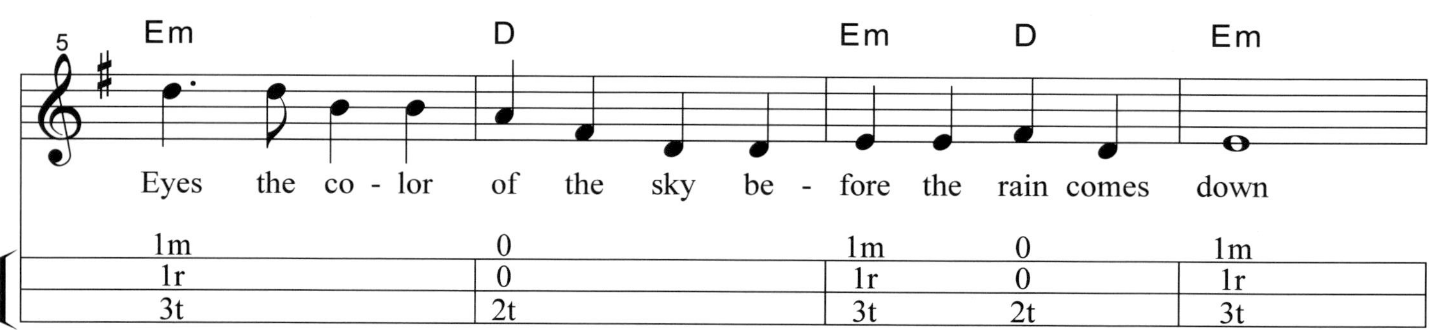

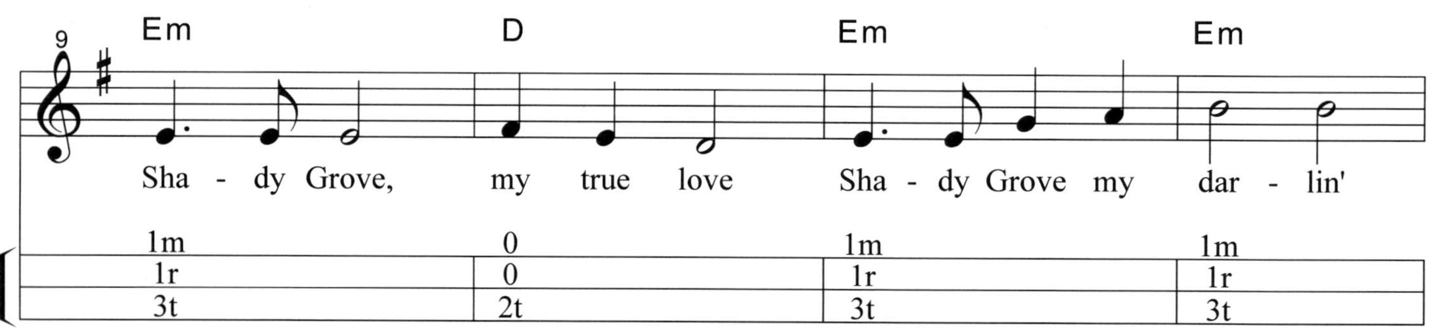

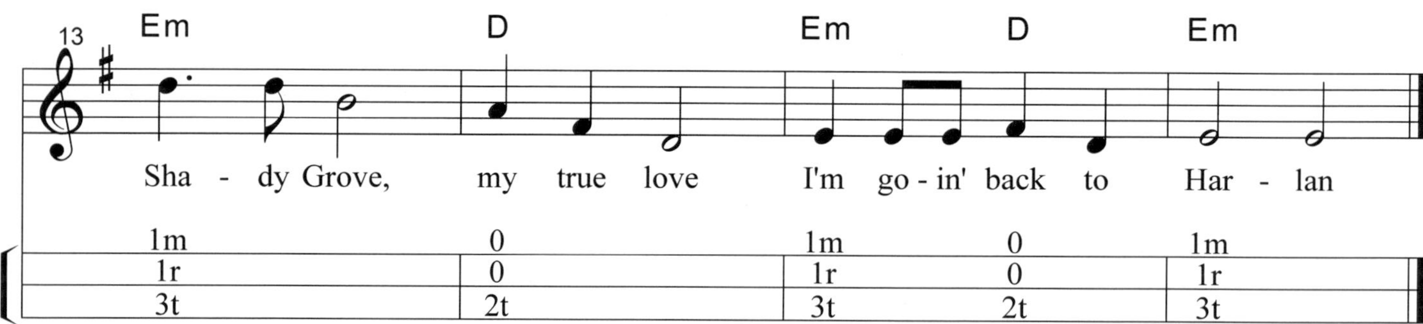

Just for fun, try playing "Shady Grove" again, this time using the "bum-did-dee" right hand strumming pattern that we worked on in the chapter about right hand techniques. A flatpick might be in order here. Play two "bum-did-dees" per measure.

This is an extra-credit challenge – if you try it, reward yourself… take yourself out to lunch! Here's the pattern – now apply it to the rest of the song.

Track 52

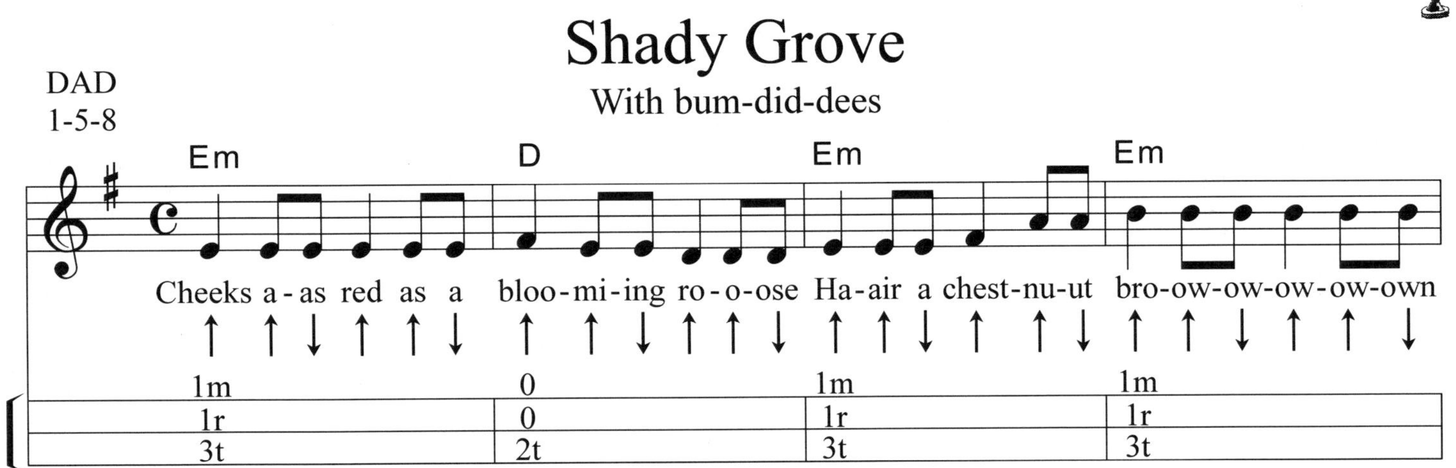

"Undefined" chords
How to cheat on the dulcimer and get away with it

Your dulcimer is tuned to DAD/DADD. That's a D chord although it's missing one note, an F♯. If you look at the three notes that make up a D chord - D, F♯ and A - you'll find that they are the first, third and fifth notes of the D scale. "What?" you say. Think of it this way:

Count on your fingers… D (one) is your thumb (just take that on faith for now), pass by E (two) on your index finger, come to F♯ (three) on your middle finger (don't worry about the "♯" – we'll get to it), pass by G (four) on your ring finger and come to A (five) on your pinkie. If you have a keyboard, play D, F♯ and A together. Sound familiar? That's a major triad: 1,3,5. This holds true for any major chord. Your starting note can be any note, but the *relationship* of the three notes will be the same.

You could also look at the D scale in the following manner. In the chart below, notice our good old "do, re, mi" scale – familiar, eh? The notes in bold type are the first, third and fifth of the scale.

Do	Re	Mi	Fa	So
1	2	**3**	4	**5**
D	E	**F♯**	G	**A**

Now here's something really important. **It's the third of the chord that tells you if the chord you're playing is a major or minor chord.** In a D chord, that's the F♯. If you strum across your dulcimer, you have only D notes and an A note – you're missing the third; the F♯. Without that third it could be either a D major *or* a D minor chord. Since you're only playing two different tones at once it's not officially a chord; it's a diad, but for our purposes we're going to call it a chord. In fact, we're going to call it an "undefined chord," which is my own name to describe a "chord" that contains only the first and the fifth of the scale.

Now, there are tons of different places on your instrument where you can play a full D chord using all three notes – the D, F♯ and A. But I really want you to get that when you strum straight across the open strings, you are playing a D chord that is missing the F♯. It can therefore be major or a minor. Here's a way for your ears to hear it:

- Press down the first string on the 2nd fret. That's an F♯ note.
- Play that note, sing it, get it in your head and then lift your finger off the string.
- Strum across your open strings and, starting with that F♯ note, sing "Three blind mice, three blind mice. See how they run, see how they run." It works, right? That song is in a major key.

Here it is written out:

Three Blind Mice

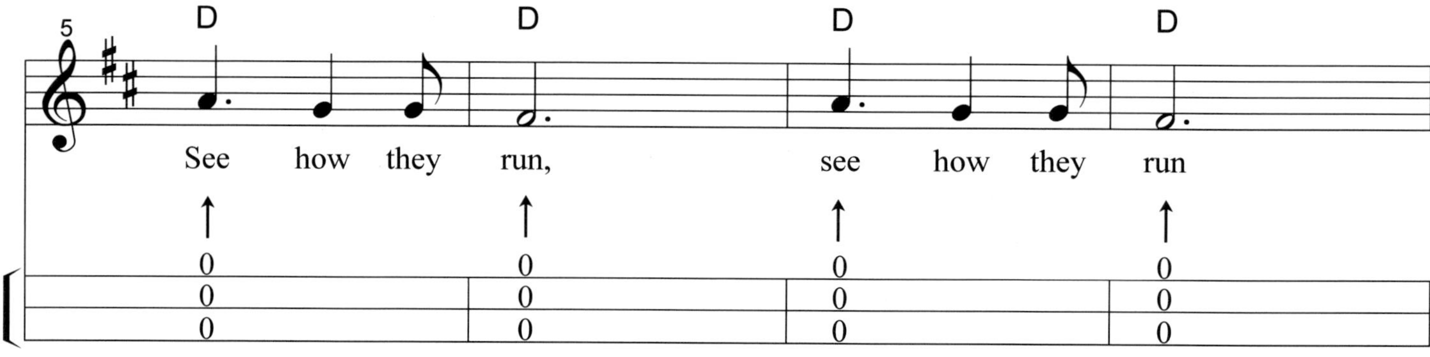

But you could swear that you're playing a minor chord if you do the following:

- Play your open first string to give yourself the starting note for the song, "God Rest Ye Merry Gentlemen."
- Strum across your open strings again and sing "God rest ye merry gentlemen, let nothing you dismay. Remember Christ our savior was born on Christmas Day."
- It works again, but this time the song is in a minor key.

And written out:

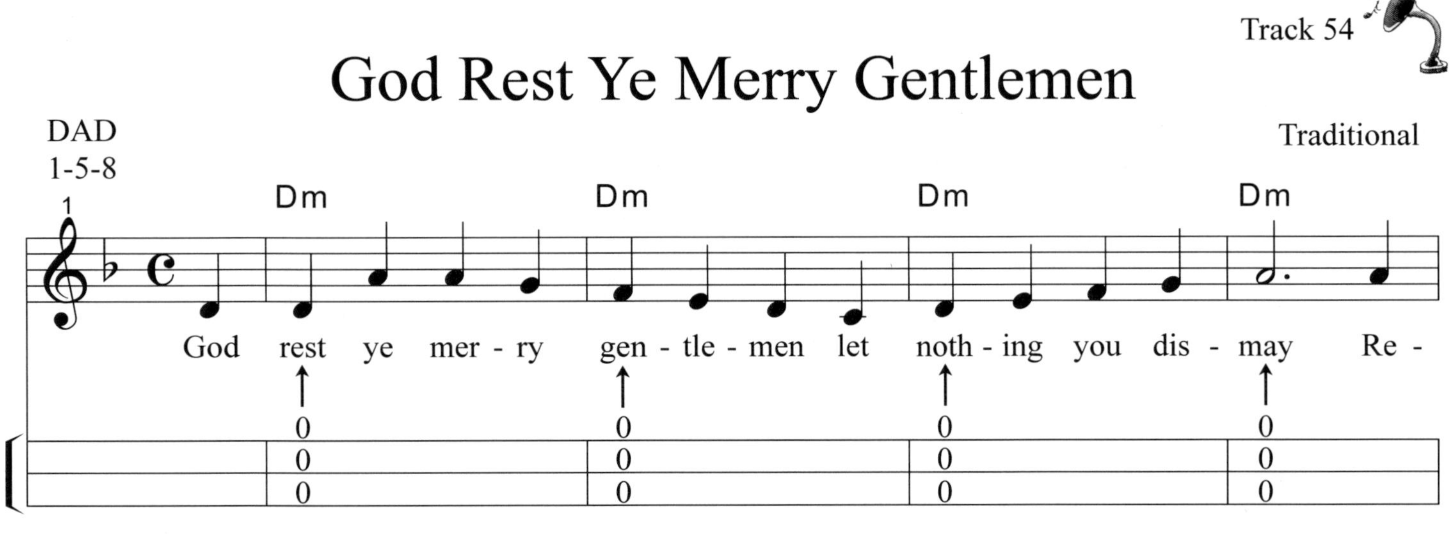

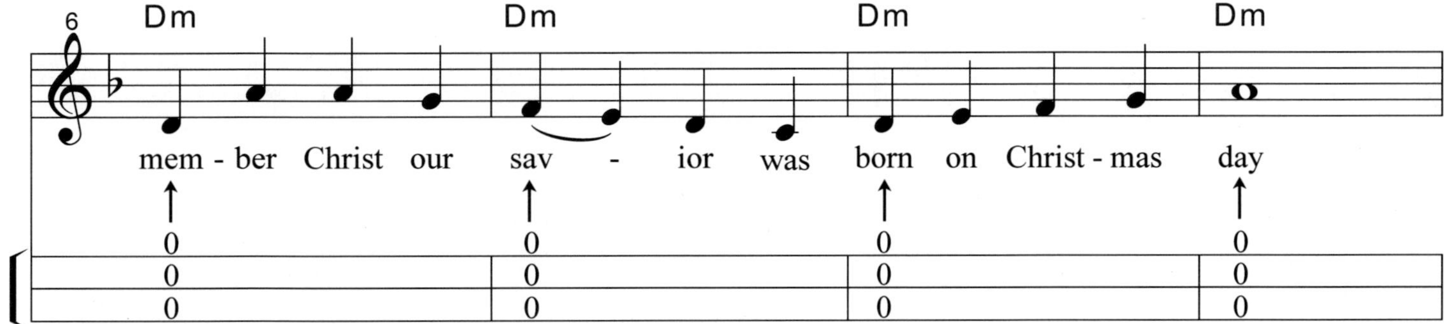

Do you hear the difference? It's kind of like a magic trick! When there's no third of the chord, you can't tell if the chord is major or minor.

Why do I think that this is so all-fired important? Because there will be times that a tune will ask for a major or a minor chord that you *can't* play because your instrument doesn't have the defining third. Without this little bit of theory, you're up the proverbial creek without a paddle.

How "undefined chords" apply to the rest of the fretboard

Try barring across the 1st fret by either placing a finger flat across the strings or by holding all the strings down with individual fingers. By applying the same theory we discussed for the D chord, you are now playing an E major *or* an E minor chord. *If you're playing with four equidistant strings, you can choose to cover all four strings, or leave the second string open. I tend to leave the second string open, as a drone, and use three fingers to cover strings one, three and four. That open string creates some interesting tonalities, but be careful: it does define a minor chord when you get to the 5th fret.*

Slide up to the 2nd fret. Now you're playing either an F♯ major *or* an F♯ minor. This concept continues right up the fretboard. Try this for yourself now by playing "Chord Chart for Undefined Chords." Pay close attention to the left hand fingering suggestions. If it feels uncomfortable as you progress, make sure that your dulcimer is seated out toward your knees and that the head stock end is angled away from you. Try and keep your fingers "rounded" so that they don't bend backwards at the knuckles. Keep your shoulders down. Enough nagging? Try these chords:

Chord Chart for "Undefined" Chords

DAD
1-5-8

D or Dm	E or Em	F♯ or F♯m	G or Gm
0	1i	2i	3i
0	1m	2m	3m
0	1r	2r	3r

A or Am	B or Bm	C or Cm	D or Dm (octave)
4i	5i	6i	7i
4m	5m	6m	7m
4r	5r	6r	7r

If you compare the "Undefined Chords" chart and the "More Chords" chart (page 72), you'll notice that the only real change is what happens on the first string. Most of the time in the "More Chords" chart, you have that defining third note of the chord "right under your thumb" – literally!

By now you've noticed that on the dulcimer, sometimes a chord appears naturally as a major, sometimes as a minor. When you're using the dulcimer as accompaniment to singing or someone else's playing, and you need a major but only have a minor (or vice versa), you can always fall back onto undefined chords. Your voice, or the melody, will supply the missing notes and no one will be the wiser… unless the melody you're playing in an instrumental incorporates a note outside the mode; [1] that's where you discover the limitations of the instrument.

---

[1] Don't know what a mode is? More about that in Book 2, Chapter 7 (The Capo).

When you have that 6½ fret you can often find a "missing" or "accidental" note on one of the strings within that group of three frets (6, 6½, and 7). On very rare occasions I find a tune I'd like to play on the dulcimer, but it just has too many accidentals (notes that are not members of the scale indicated by the key signature). But I don't give up often!

Lots more chords

Here's one last chart (pages 80-81) that contains the chords that I use on a regular basis and that I find most "user friendly."

Take a look at the first system and observe that a D chord can be played as 0,0,2 or as 2,0,0. That's because your bass string and your first string are both D notes (an octave apart), so you're playing an inversion of the same chord. The same applies to the following "pairs":
- 0,0,4 and 4,0,0
- 0,3,2 and 2,3,0
- 0,5,4 and 4,5,0

Now, did you notice that I included 4,5,7 in the chart but not 7,5,4? Why? Excellent question. Try 7,5,4. Question answered? I left it out because although 7,5,4 *is* a D chord, I can't play it. You'll find this same concept throughout the chart. If you've got fingers that will stretch to form the inversions I left out, go for it!

I've included fingering suggestions for some, but not all the chords on this chart, as there are some chords that you'll need to finger in different ways, depending upon where they appear in the tune you're playing. Where you see left-hand suggestions, you can assume that I play them consistently with that fingering.

When you see a "u" over the chord, it means that the chord is "undefined" – it doesn't contain the defining third of the chord – so it can be used as a major or a minor chord.

Chord Chart
DAD/1-5-8

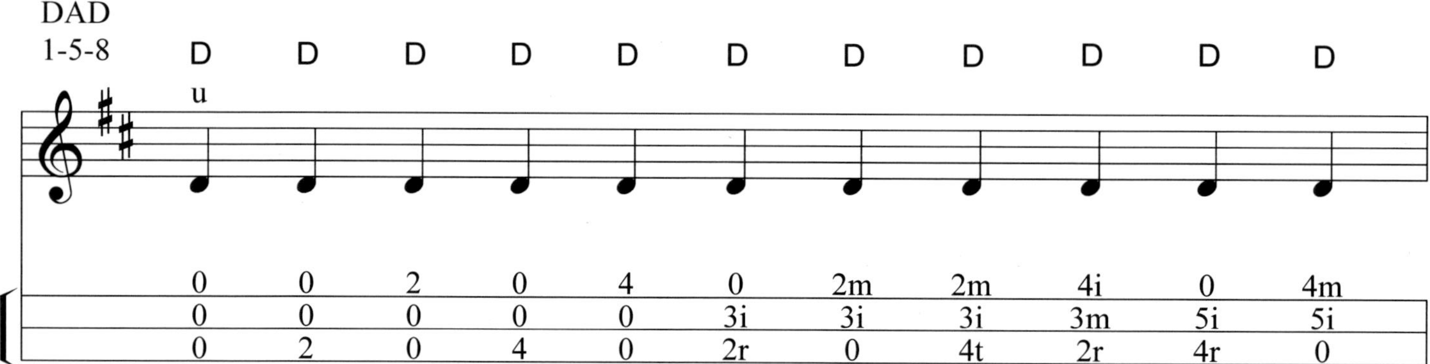

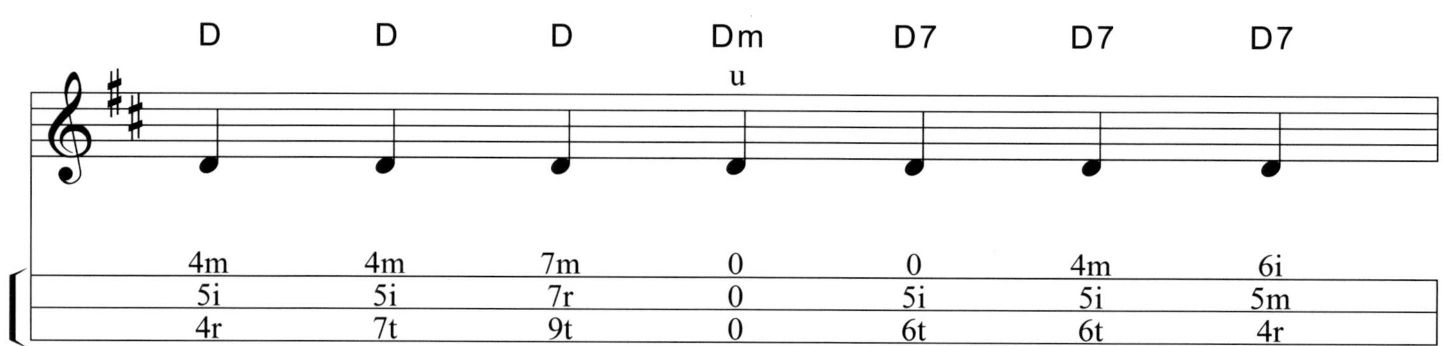

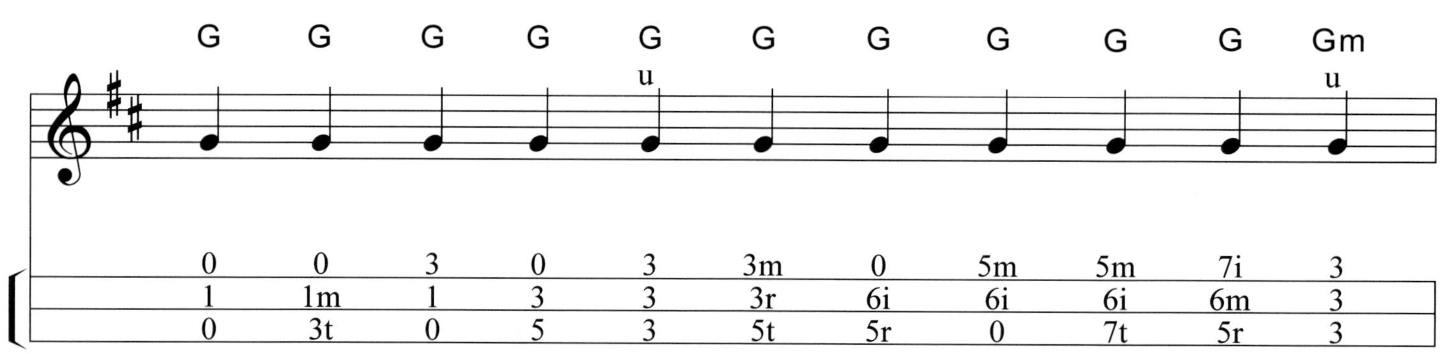

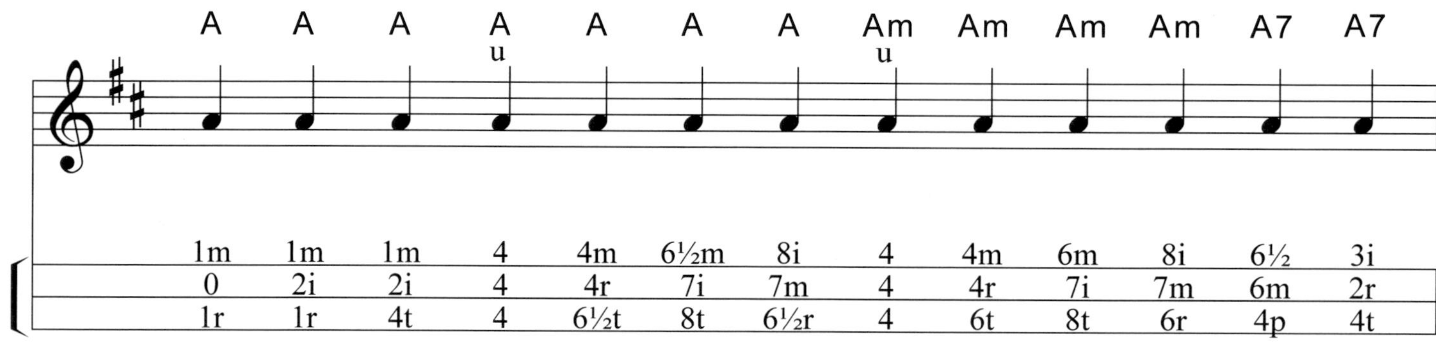

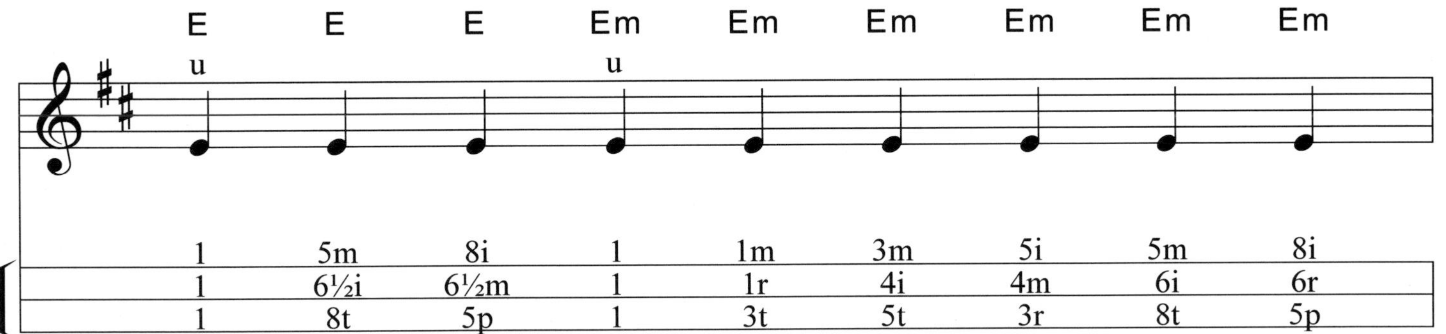

E   E   E   Em   Em   Em   Em   Em   Em
u   u
1   5m   8i   1   1m   3m   5i   5m   8i
1   6½i   6½m   1   1r   4i   4m   6i   6r
1   8t   5p   1   3t   5t   3r   8t   5p

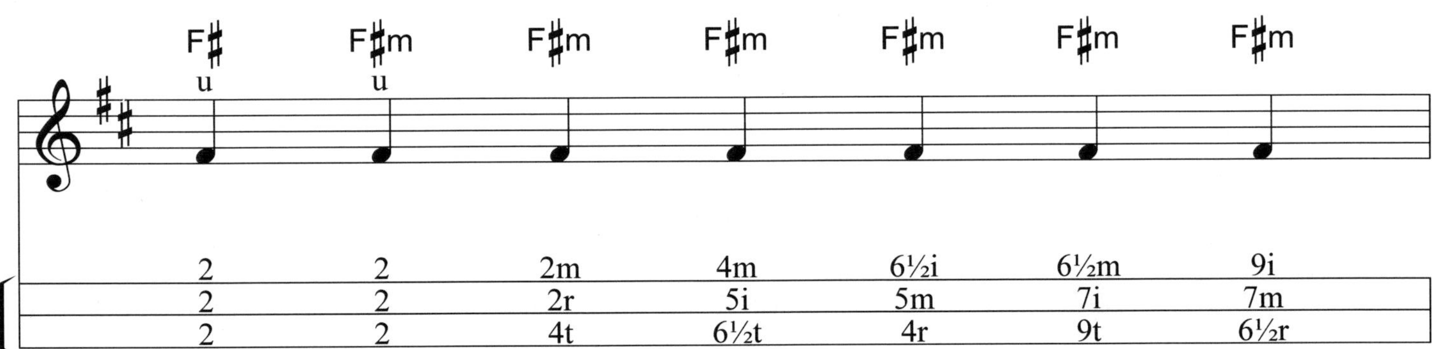

F♯   F♯m   F♯m   F♯m   F♯m   F♯m   F♯m
u   u
2   2   2m   4m   6½i   6½m   9i
2   2   2r   5i   5m   7i   7m
2   2   4t   6½t   4r   9t   6½r

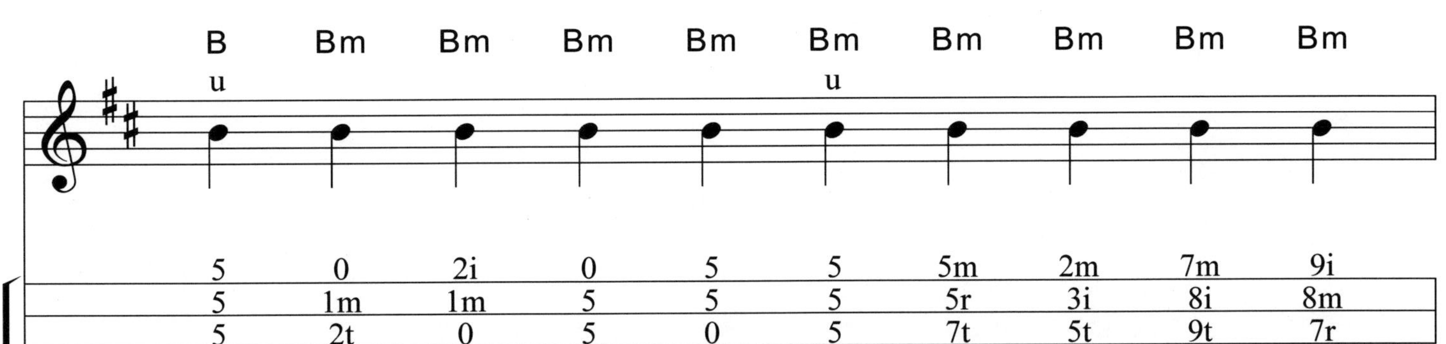

B   Bm   Bm   Bm   Bm   Bm   Bm   Bm   Bm   Bm
u   u
5   0   2i   0   5   5   5m   2m   7m   9i
5   1m   1m   5   5   5   5r   3i   8i   8m
5   2t   0   5   0   5   7t   5t   9t   7r

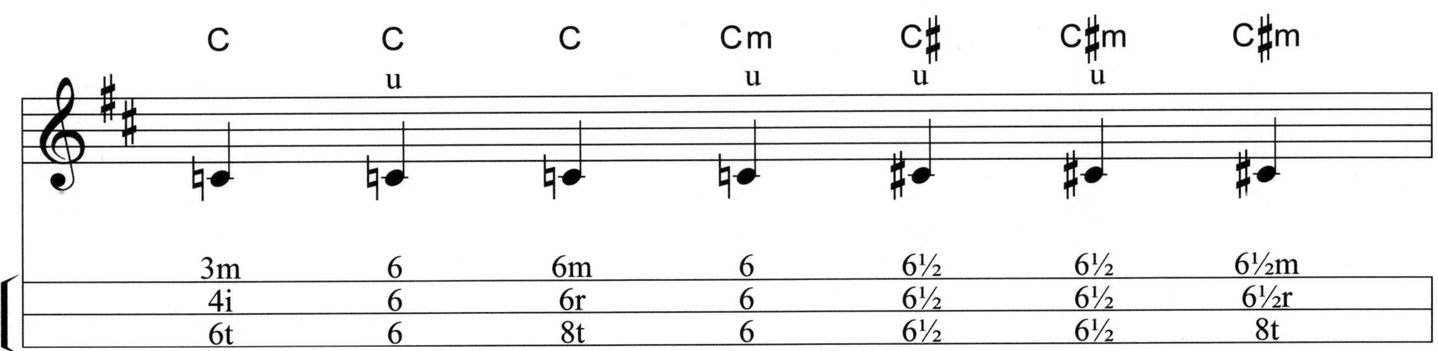

C   C   C   Cm   C♯   C♯m   C♯m
u   u   u   u
3m   6   6m   6   6½   6½   6½m
4i   6   6r   6   6½   6½   6½r
6t   6   8t   6   6½   6½   8t

Recognizing – and memorizing – chords

Most of my students seem to resist learning the names and placements of basic chords. I don't expect you to know every chord that you play on the dulcimer. Frankly, *I* don't – especially when I go into tunings other than DAD/DADD. But a good working knowledge, and the ability to find and recognize basic chords quickly, will take you a long way.

There's only so much I can do to help you in the memorizing department – you either do it or you don't. But I *can* give you some guidance as to how to go about it, and what chords seem to me to be the most important to have right at your fingertips.

Since your dulcimer is tuned to a D chord, it's good to know a few of them. If I were you, these are the ones on which I would concentrate:

1. 0,0,0
2. 0,0,2
3. 0,3r,2i
4. 0,5r,4i

All four of these D chords are readily accessible no matter what position you're playing in. They're well balanced (with just a hint of oak) and you'll find that you use them often.

For the following chords, there's an easy way to figure out what chord you're playing. Think of the alphabet, then follow the chords right up the fretboard, using the same fingering that is indicated for the Em. They are mostly the chords that you played in the chart called "More Chords."

1. Em = 1m,1r,3t
2. F$\sharp$m = 2,2,4
3. G = 3,3,5
4. Am = 4,4,6
5. A = 4,4,6½
6. Bm = 5,5,7
7. C = 6,6,8

That will help you locate the chords, but it's still up to you to learn to recognize them as you use them, without having to "count" up the fretboard. Yes, I really do think you should make a stab at memorizing them. Investing the time now in learning at least one form of each chord is like learning the notes on the musical staff. In the long run, it will save you time and aggravation.

In this book I only include the chords I frequently use in the tunings that I use the most. If you're looking for more, there are many books available with extensive chord charts in many different tunings. You can also look online. In your own playing you may find other chords that you use more often that you'll memorize as you go along.

You have not seen the last of chords; we'll be using them in all kinds of ways throughout this book and in Book 2. In fact, in the next chapter, we'll create instrumentals by combining some of those chords you just learned with basic right hand techniques.

Chapter 6 ~ Combining Chords with Basic Right Hand Techniques
Putting it all together

This is a short chapter in terms of instruction, but it's an important one – sort of a bridge from the basics to actually playing your instrument. It's the point where you get to take all those seemingly unrelated exercises and chords and make them work together.

Let's start out with a familiar tune, "Clementine." Notice the chord names above the staff. Those are the chords you're playing within the structure of the TAB.

- With your right hand you do exactly what you did when you were learning about right hand techniques.
- The arrows indicate the direction of the strum, which I suggest you do with your right index finger.
- Use your right thumb for the notes that appear on the first string and use whatever finger is comfortable to you for the bass and middle strings. *A reminder for those of you with four equidistant strings: leave that second string open – just let it ring out.*

Clementine

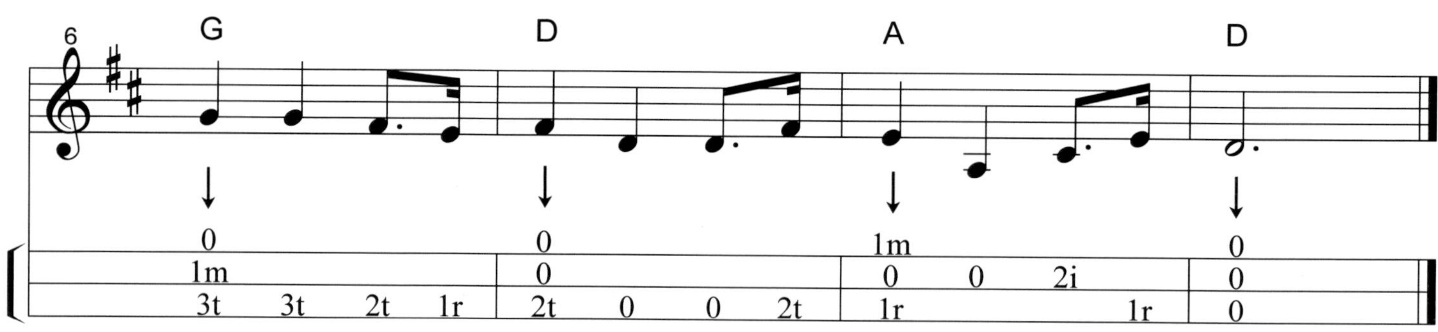

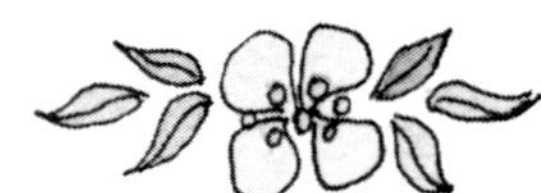

For "Matt's Return":

- Keep the fingering consistent but take note of the difference in measures #2 and #4. The finger you use for the final note of each of those measures depends on what you have to do in the measure that follows.
- When you get to measure #5, watch the fingering of the G chord (3,3,3). If you're playing the correct fingering in measure #4, you'll be fine.

Matt's Return

©2015 Anne Dodson

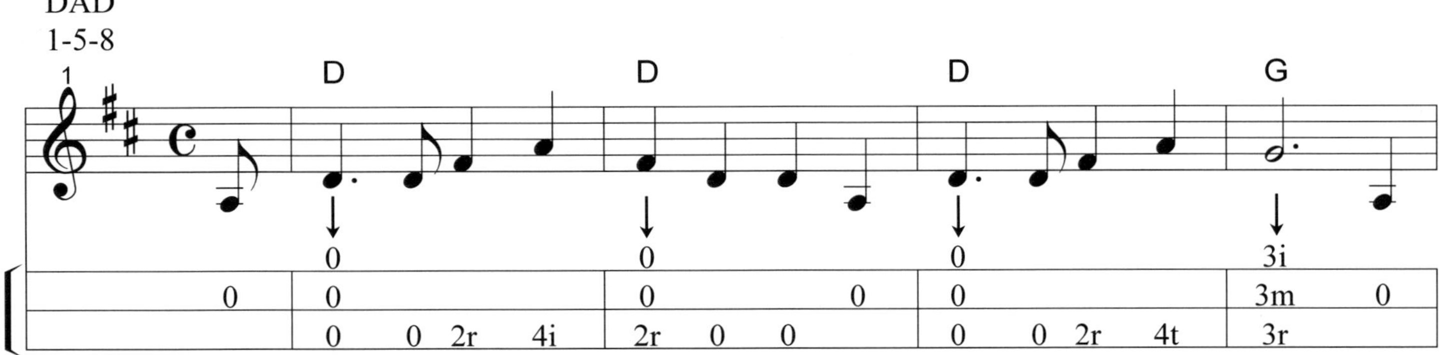

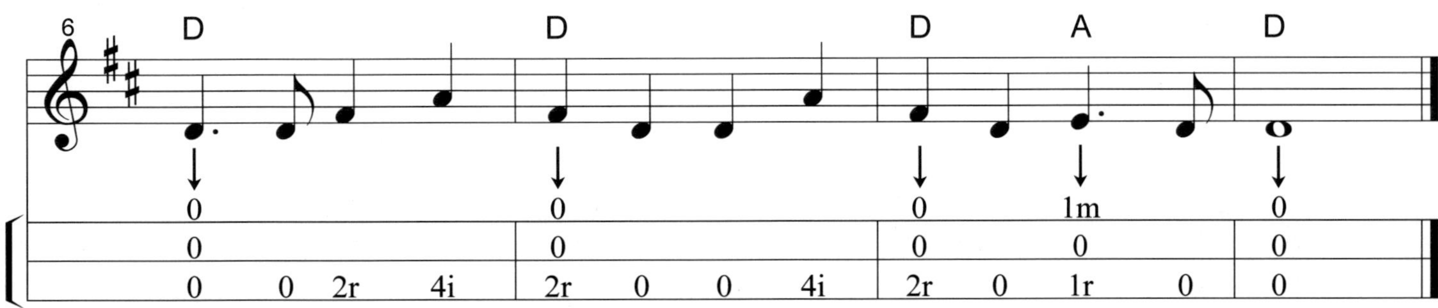

Throughout this book I generally leave it up to you to guess why the tunes are named as they are. However, "Deest and Cheest" is such a distinctive title that people always ask what it means, so I'll fill you in.

I had two young students who came together for lessons. One of them had a horse named "Destry" and the other had a chicken named "Chester." "Deest and Cheest" were the animals' nicknames. I wrote this tune for the girls, so I asked them to give it a name and this is what they came up with.

There are three sections - A1, A2 and A3. The melody is the same in each of them, but you'll notice that the TAB is different. Here's what's happening:
- A1 uses no specific chords except those D chords that are formed with the open middle and bass strings.
- A2 uses chords that are similar to many of the chords you just learned – you're just leaving your middle string open to create a nice open sound.
- A3 uses some of those complete chords that you worked so hard to learn and recognize.

Strum with your right index finger, and remember to use the appropriate finger or thumb for single notes. Pay attention to the timing.

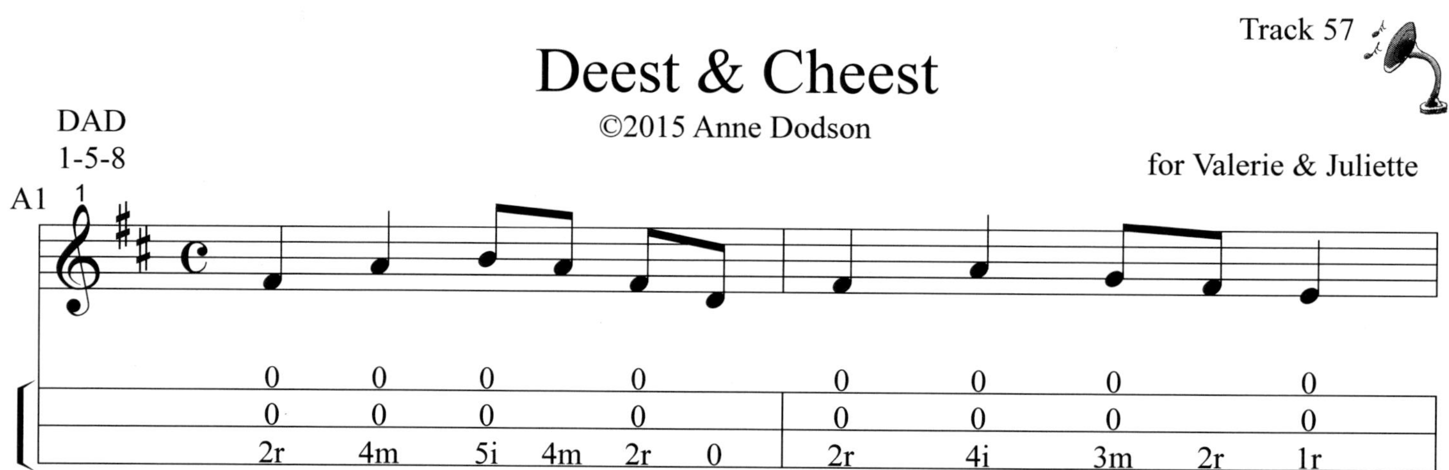

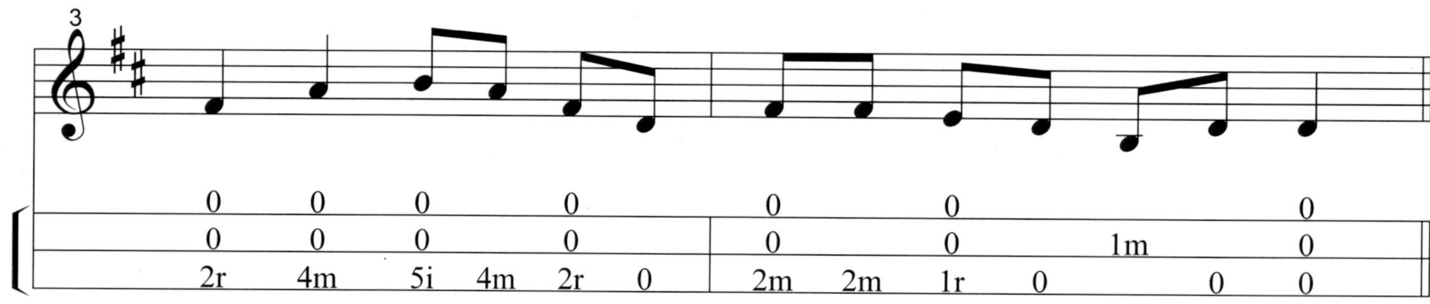

Deest & Cheest

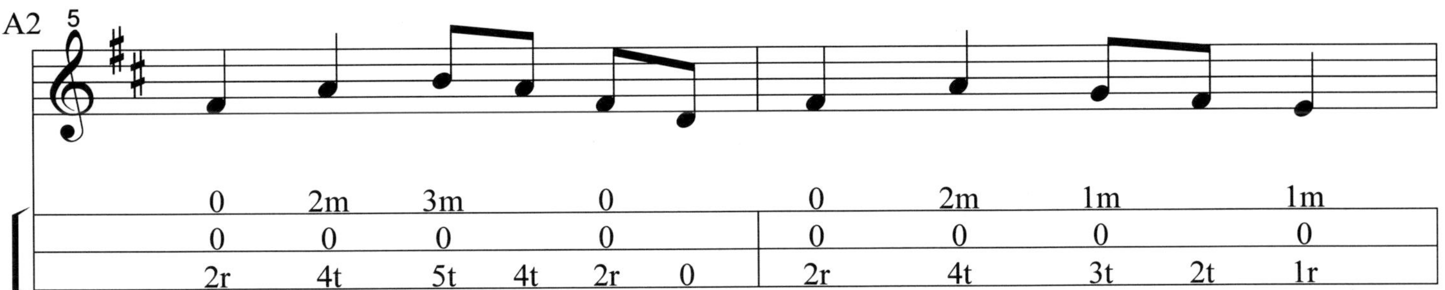

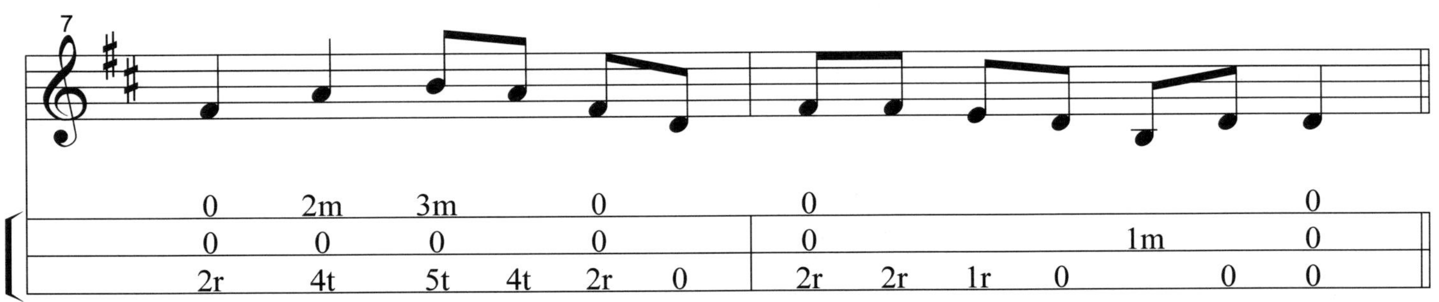

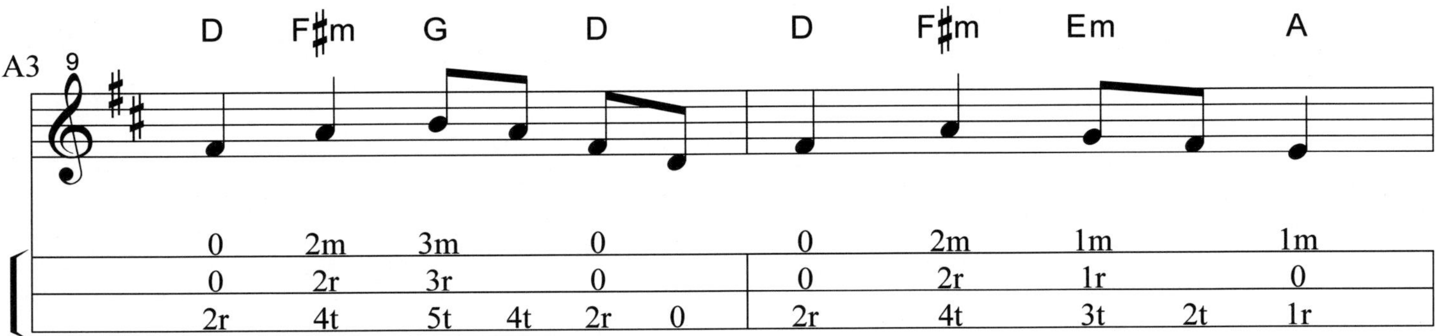

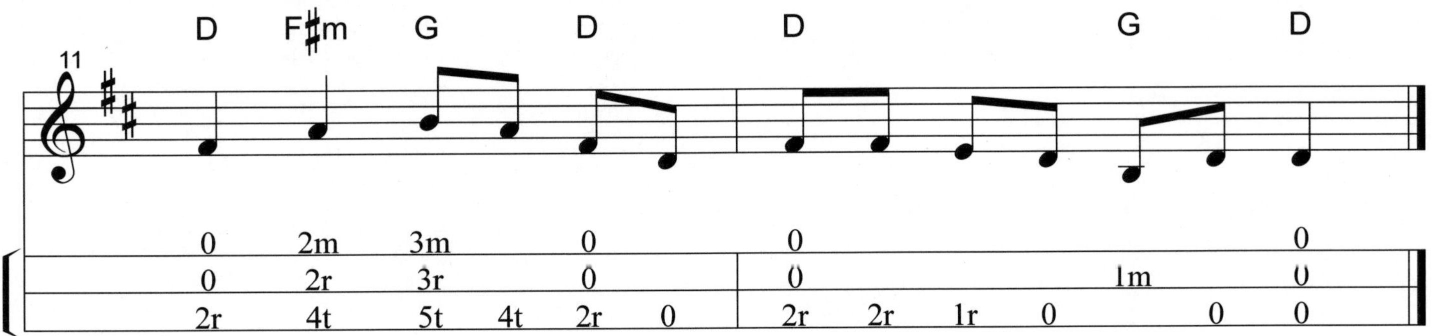

Did you prefer one of the three versions? To my ears, they all have merit, although I think I prefer A2. It sort of "hints" at the chords, but leaves an open, almost traditional sound. You can play it any way you like, or even combine versions.

In "Jessie the Cat" you get to combine strumming, picking and plucking, just as you did in the chapter about basic right hand techniques. Here's a refresher: if you see arrows, strum the chord in the direction of the arrow; pick single notes with an appropriate finger; if there are two notes together, pluck them with thumb and finger.

Jessie the Cat

©2015 Anne Dodson

For Nancy & David

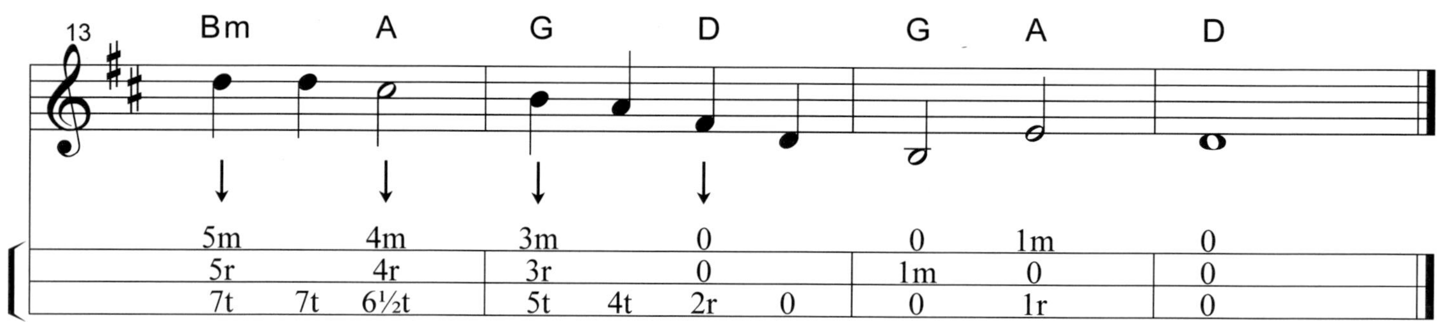

Here are two more tunes for you to try. Although I've included left hand fingering suggestions, I have purposely left out specific instructions for your right hand. You're on your own – strum, pluck and pick away! Have fun with it. With "Lament," take a look at measures #10 and #14. The fingering change is a variation – not a typo!

Lament

©2015 Anne Dodson

And a waltz – three beats to the measure. If you count out the timing before you begin playing, you'll find yourself ahead of the game.

Far Away

©2015 Anne Dodson

I hope that this chapter was the payoff that you'd been patiently waiting for. Next, we move on to some new adventures for your left hand.

Chapter 7 ~ Basic Left Hand Techniques
Pull-offs, hammer-ons and slides

Slides, hammer-ons and pull-offs are left-hand techniques that allow you to play more fluidly and can increase your speed for playing fast tunes. Use my suggested fingering as a guideline but feel free to experiment, as people seem to have very strong, and very different, opinions about fingering for hammer-ons, pull-offs and slides. My fingers are small and not remarkably strong, so I'm relatively conservative in how I use my left hand. That is reflected in my suggestions. If your fingers are happy making more "aggressive" runs, or you are comfortable using your left pinkie, then by all means, modify the fingering. Go for it!

If you feel that you've got too many new things going on at one time, you can play through any of these tunes without the hammer-ons, pull-offs and slides. Add them when you feel better acquainted with the notes and the timing.

For this chapter, "pluck" describes the picking of a single string with just one finger of either hand.

Pull-offs

Among left hand techniques, pull-offs seem to be the easiest for most people, so that's where we'll start. Basically, all you're doing with a pull-off is picking the note with your left hand instead of your right hand.
- Put any left-hand finger on the first string of the 1st fret.
- Now just pluck the string with your left hand. It won't work to just lift your finger – you actually have to play it.
- Pull up and pluck slightly toward you, all in one motion. You are simply playing the note with any left hand finger instead of using your right hand as you normally would to pluck a string.
- I repeat: use your left hand only for this exercise.

Track 61 

Pull-off #1

DAD
1-5-8

You may find that it's hard to get an even sound each time, (unless you're a left-handed player, playing the instrument right-handed. Then you're really excited!). Play it a few times until you feel that you've got some control. Just for fun, try plucking the middle string and the bass string in the same manner.

Once you've gotten the feel of using your left hand to pluck, you're ready to integrate it into your playing. Look at the next exercise while you:
- Place your left middle finger on the first string of the 1st fret and press down.
- Remember to press down right behind the fret.

- Now strike that first string with your right hand as you usually would.
- *Then* pull-off with your left hand so that you get two notes in succession (the "E" pulls-off to the open "D" note).
- Notice that you are playing two different notes, the first being plucked with your right hand, the second being plucked with your left hand.
- Each time you go back to the "E" note on the 1st fret, you need to set your finger back down and pull-off to the open "D."
- You'll notice that a pull-off is indicated in the TAB by a slur with a "p" under the slur.
- Keep in mind that the *movement* of the pull-off creates the second note – that can confuse you when you look at the tablature. Go ahead – try it.

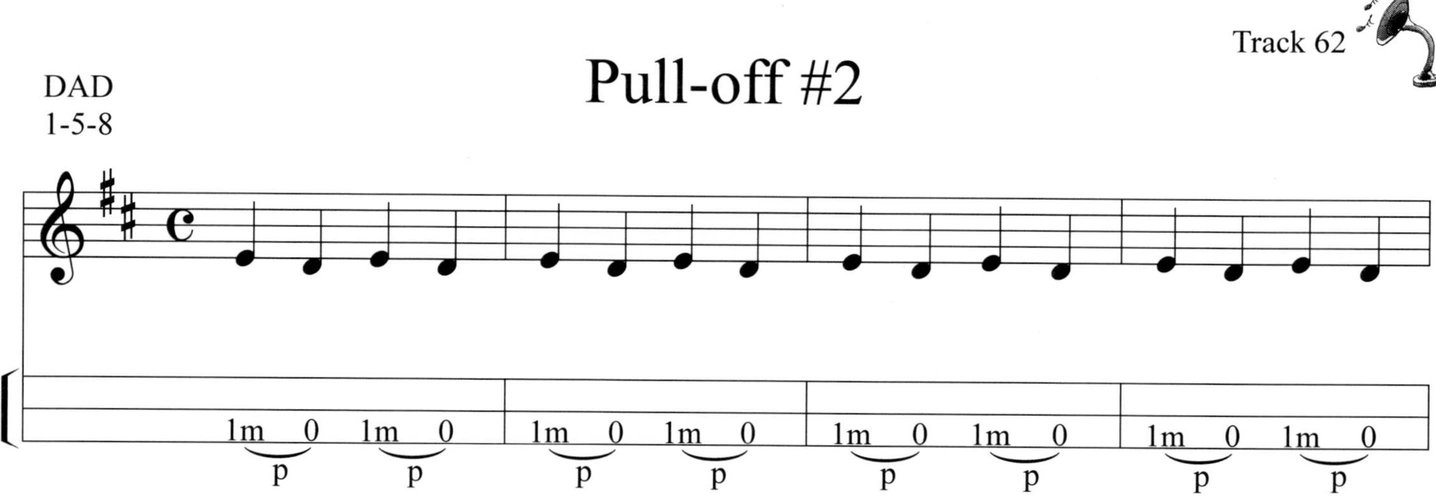

Okay – this time you're going to do the same thing you did in the last exercise, but you're going to play it first on the first string, then on your middle string, then on the bass string, etc.

- Use your left middle finger this time through.
- Remember that you play the first note with your right hand; the second note is a pull-off to the open string, done with your left hand.
- Having fun yet? It takes some time to get comfortable with the idea of using your left hand to do some of the plucking. Your brain may resist for a while. Give it some time to get those connections going, and be patient. (Perhaps I should write, "be patient" at the top of each page of this book?).

Now try that same exercise (pull-off #3), but do the pull-offs with your left index finger. Then, repeat with your ring finger.

Now, here's a really fun part. This is just too good. Here's what you do:
- Place your left-hand index finger on the first string, 2nd fret.
- Now put your left-hand ring finger on the first string, 1st fret.
- You're about to play two pull-offs in succession, so it's really important that you keep both fingers down on the fretboard. Think of the first two measures of "Three Blind Mice."
- With those fingers in position, take your *right* hand and pluck that first string.
- Now take your right hand out of action and pull-off with your left-hand index finger.
- Your left-hand ring finger should still be in place on the first string, 1st fret.
- Now pull-off with your ring finger. You *do not* pluck with your right hand for the pull-offs. You only use your right hand to pluck the string at the beginning of each measure.
- The notes you'll be playing will be F♯, E, D.
- You're ready to start, but first put *both fingers* down as a unit and keep them in position until you do the pull-offs.

Track 64

Pull-off #4

DAD
1-5-8

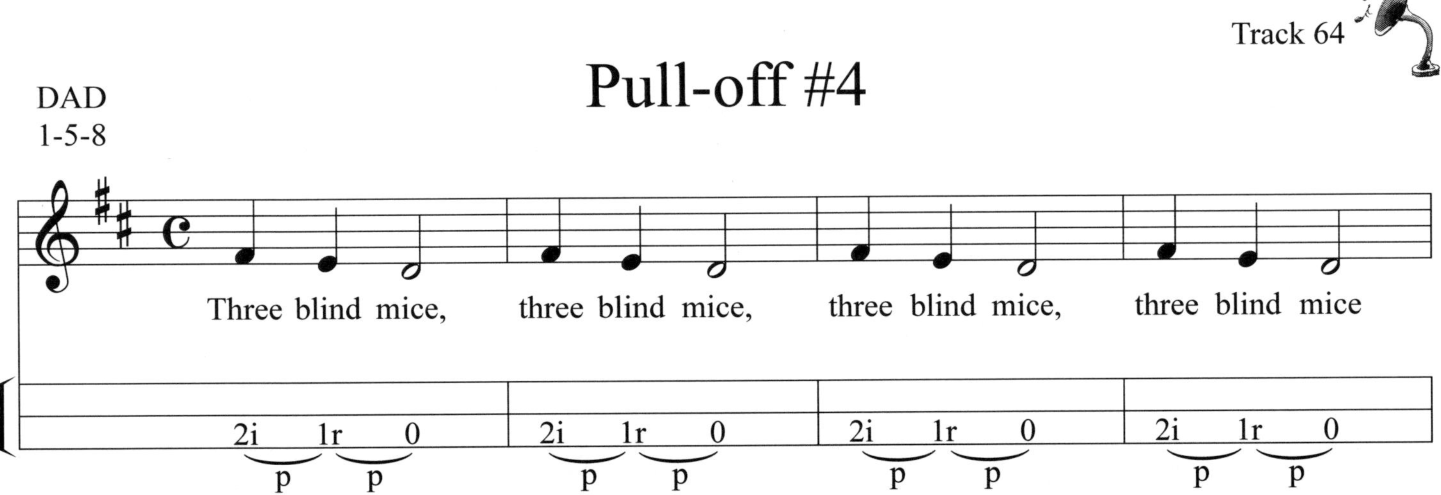

Did you feel as if you needed to play the pull-offs really fast? Many people think they have to move quickly. With pull-offs, you have all the time in the world between notes. As you do these pull-off exercises, work toward making them fluid and try to keep a consistent tempo. Speeding them up will come with practice.

Now try the same pull-offs, with the same fingering, on your middle string, and then on your bass string – like this:

Track 65

Pull-off #5

DAD
1-5-8

In the last two exercises I gave you some space to make the transitions between strings by giving you a half note after two quarter notes. Sometimes you'll use this timing in tunes, but more likely you'll need to move between the strings more quickly. In this next line you move to 3/4 time (waltz time), where you'll need to get from one string to the other without the luxury of a half note to give you time to think before moving to a new string.

- Play as slowly as you need to, keeping the beat regular.
- Only speed up when you are able to play without pauses between the phrases.
- Remember to place both your index and ring fingers on the fretboard before you start each phrase. Think "Fi-ga-ro, Fi-ga-ro."
- Strike the note with your right hand only once per measure.

Track 66

Pull-off #6

DAD
1-5-8

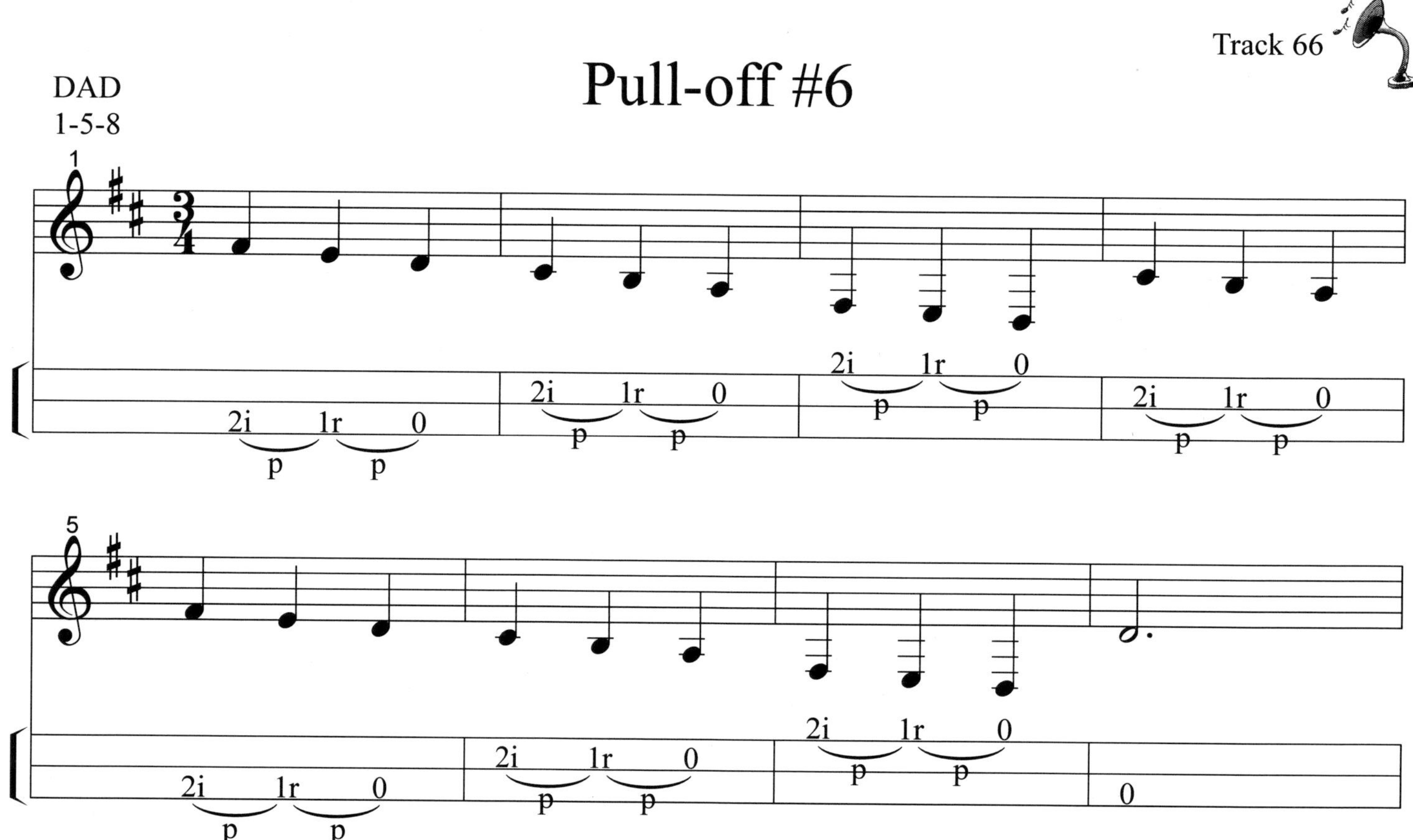

Hammer-ons

When you feel you've got a handle on pull-offs, then it's time to move on to hammer-ons. Hammer-ons are just what the name implies. Like pull-offs, you use your left hand to play two or more consecutive notes, but instead of pulling off to play a lower note, you bring your finger down on a fret to play a higher note.

Here's what you do:
- Play your first string open with your right hand.
- Then with a firm, controlled motion bring the middle finger of your left hand down onto the first string, 1st fret. You actually have to hammer it on with some force.
- You'll find that if you just place your finger down, you get a mute – not a second note. It may take a little practice to get the right combination of force and accuracy.
- Keep your hand level, with your fingers rounded and close to the fretboard. Make sure you're coming down on the note just behind the fret.
- The temptation is to panic and hammer-on too quickly. You've got time.
- Experiment until you get two clear notes.
- Hammer-ons are notated in the TAB with an "h."

You'll find that I usually suggest that you use your middle finger for single pull-offs and hammer-ons in these exercises. That's because my middle finger is my strongest left-hand finger. Use whatever finger works best for you, but make sure you pay attention to suggested fingering for consecutive note runs.

Track 67

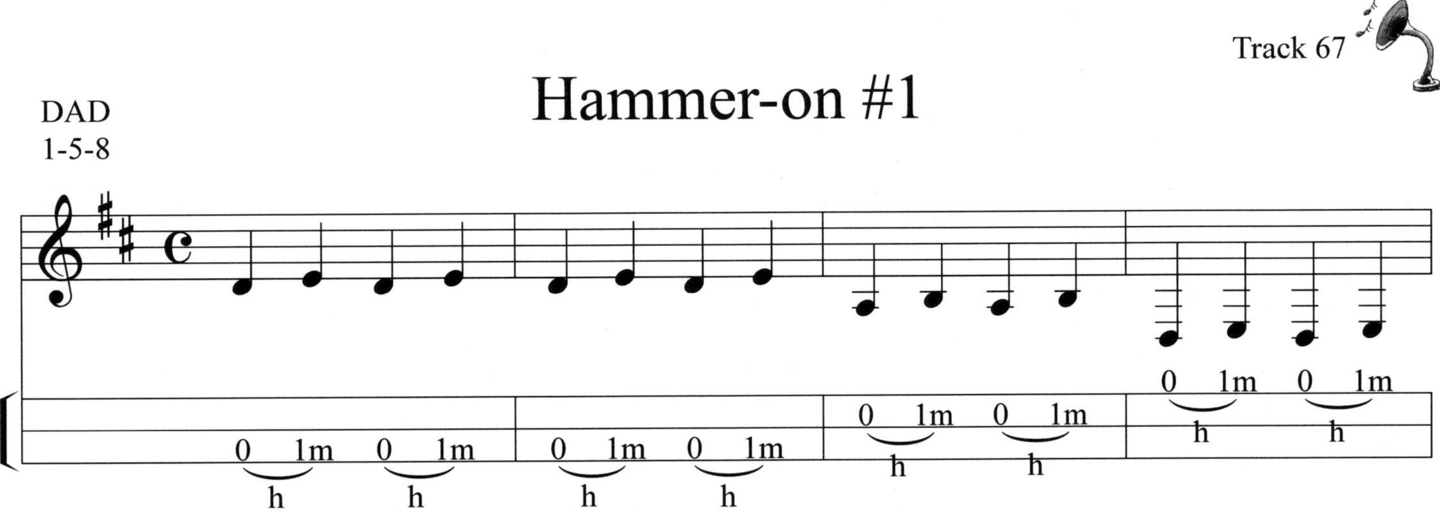

You can also hammer-on to a note that is more than just one note higher.

Track 68

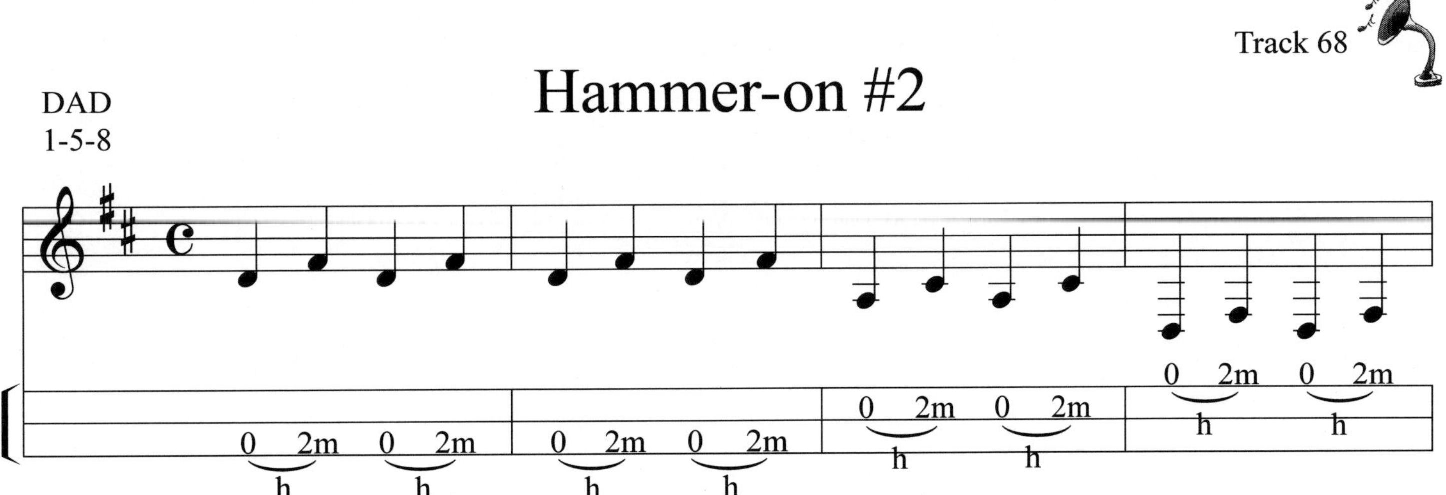

As with pull-offs, you can play more than two notes in a row. Here's an exercise in which you play three notes, two of which are created by hammer-ons.

- Take a deep breath.
- Play your first string, open, with your right hand.
- Hammer-on to the 1st fret with your left-hand ring finger.
- Then do a second hammer-on with your left-hand index finger onto the 2nd fret.
- Only pluck once with your right hand at the beginning of each measure.

The temptation will be to do them fast. You have more time than you think you do. The key is control and accuracy.

- Once you've played the first hammer-on, try to keep the ring finger (your "back" finger) of your left hand in place on the string. In all likelihood, it will want to rise up when you do the second hammer-on with your index finger.
- Don't let it have its way!

Hammer-on #3

As with pull-offs, I gave you a little space to transfer from one sequence to the next with that half note at the end of each measure. This time, try the same fingering, but in 3/4 time, so that you don't hesitate between phrases. Do it as slowly as you need to, so that you create an even beat.

Hammer-on #4

Combining hammer-ons and pull-offs

Combining hammer-ons and pull-offs in the same phrase is when it gets really interesting… and fun. Try this:

Track 71

Hammer-on / Pull-off Exercise #1

Now try the same exercise, but add some bass plucks. I've also added another hammer-on and another pull-off to the final measure where, yes, there are two hammer-ons in succession!

Track 72

Hammer-on / Pull-off Exercise #2

You have officially graduated from the school of hammer-ons and pull-offs – congratulations! It's time to try it with a complete tune. "Megunticook Rising" was written as the river next to my mom's house was… well, rising. Watch out – it's in 6/8 timing. If you find the timing to be a challenge, clap out the rhythm before you begin to play.

Track 73

Megunticook Rising

©2015 Anne Dodson

DAD
1-5-8

Here's a new technique to prepare you for "Asha's Jig." It's a hammer-on, pull-off sequence.

- Place your ring finger on the first string, 2nd fret.
- Keep it there – don't let it rise up when you…
- Hammer-on to the 3rd fret with your index finger.
- Now pull-off with your index finger.
- Your ring finger should still be in place on the 2nd fret.

Track 74

Hammer-on / Pull-off Exercise #3

DAD
1-5-8

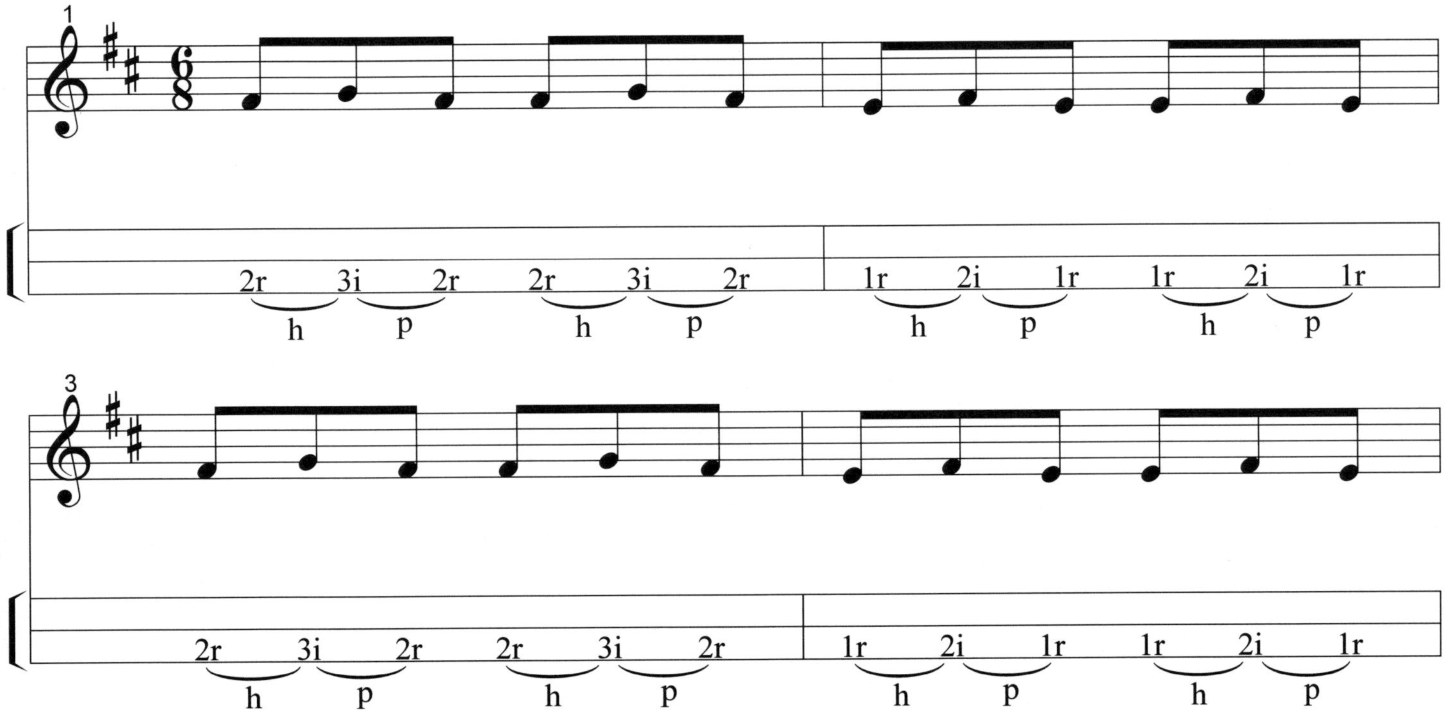

You can move this sequence to other places on the fretboard as well.

I wrote "Asha's Jig" while giving my friend Asha a lesson on hammer-ons & pull-offs. Measures #3, #7, #9 and #10 all include the technique that you just learned.

Slides

I use slides a lot (indicated in the TAB with an "s"). They are yet another left-hand method of getting from one fret to another, and they create a wonderful sound. Here's what you do:

- Place your left middle finger on the first string, 1st fret.
- Pluck that note with your right hand and then quickly and with confidence, slide your left finger up to the 2nd fret.
- You need to keep the pressure down with that finger. Lifting it, even a little, will mute the string.
- You have time between striking the note and sliding, but once you begin the slide, it needs to go fast, and you need to move it all the way up to just behind the 2nd fret.
- Most people tend to panic and rush into the slide, which creates a "galloping horse" rhythm (you may have done the same thing when you started playing hammer-ons).
- You can slide within a basic, consistent timing but – I repeat myself here because it's important – once you start the sliding motion you need to do it quickly, accurately and with conviction!
- Don't go lifting that finger. Experiment to see how much downward pressure you need to keep the note clear.

Track 76

Slides #1

DAD
1-5-8

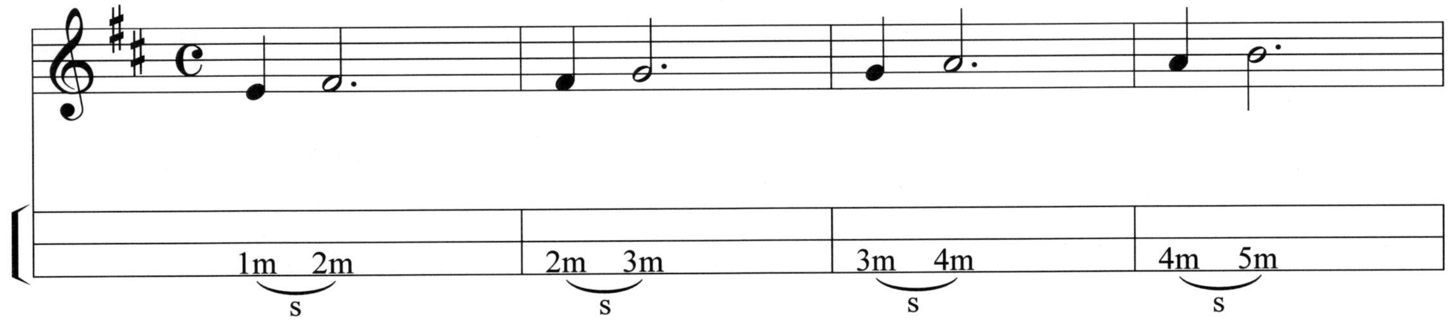

Now try sliding on the other strings.

Track 77

Slides #2

DAD
1-5-8

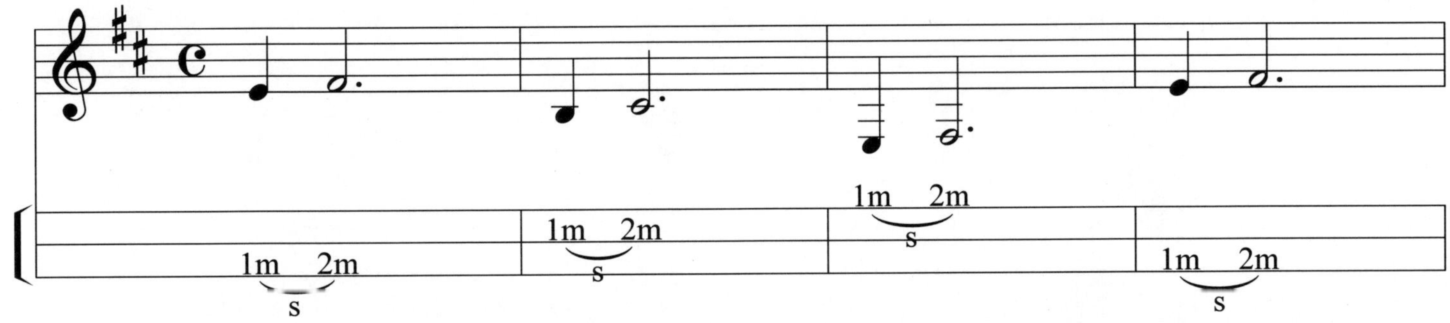

You can slide down too. The same rules apply – move swiftly when you move, don't let up pressure on the string, and end up just behind your "goal" fret.

Slides #3

DAD
1-5-8

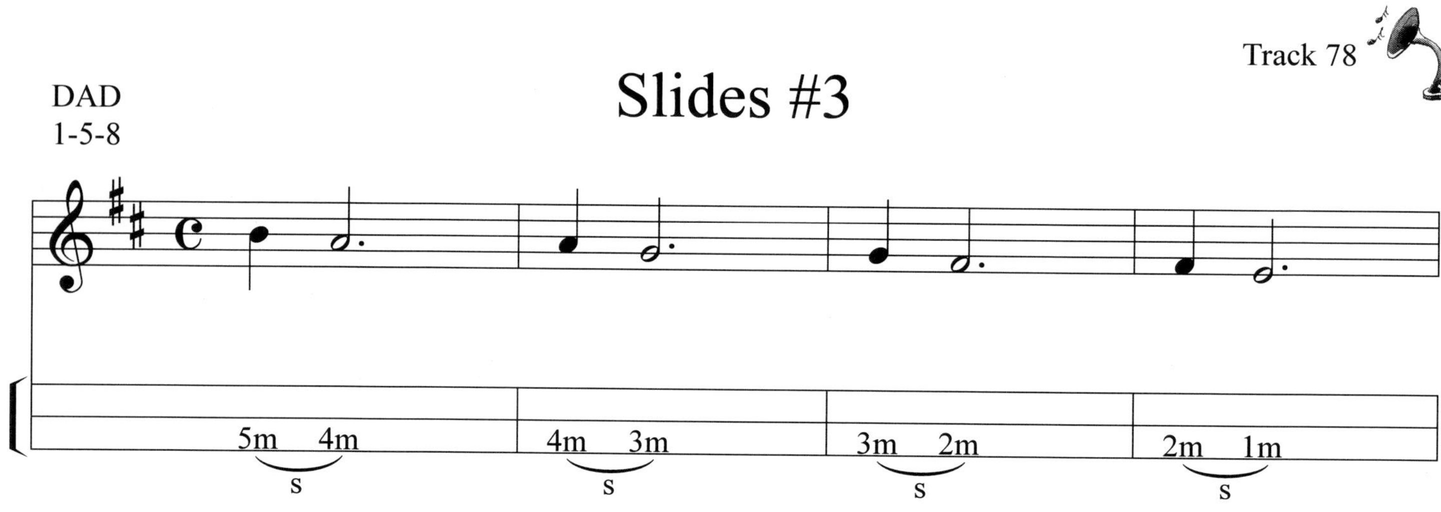

And of course, you can slide on any string.

Slides #4

DAD
1-5-8

Now go back through all four slide exercises, but this time, try leading with your wrist. Here's what I mean:
- When you slide up the fretboard, cock your wrist, ever so slightly to the right, so that your hand falls back, ever so slightly, to the left – your wrist leads the way (first photo).
- When you slide *down* the fretboard, you do the opposite – your wrist now leads to the left (second photo).
- The angle of the wrist may look more obvious sliding up than sliding down.

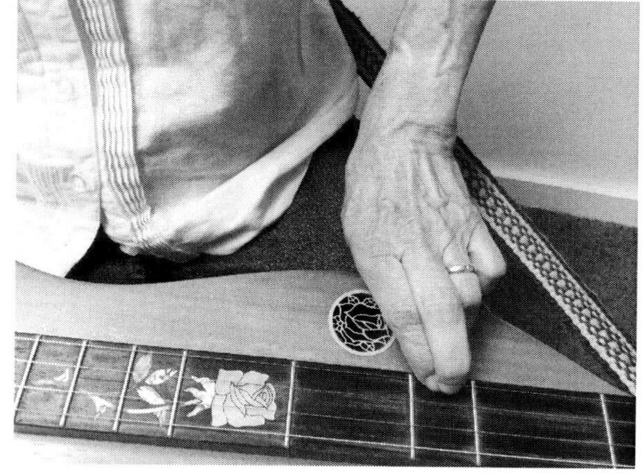

Slide up…

Slide down…

Here's a tune with a couple of slides for you to try.

Trillium Way

©2015 Anne Dodson

For Christine & Dennis

That gives you a general picture of what slides are about. You'll continue with slides as we move on to exercises and tunes that combine hammer-ons, pull-offs and slides.

Combining hammer-ons, pull-offs and slides

You've had some experience now with combining hammer-ons and pull-offs. In the following exercise you add slides to the mix. You'll notice that I don't suggest left hand fingering. Try playing it a number of times using different left-hand fingers. Remember to strike the first note of each measure with your right hand.

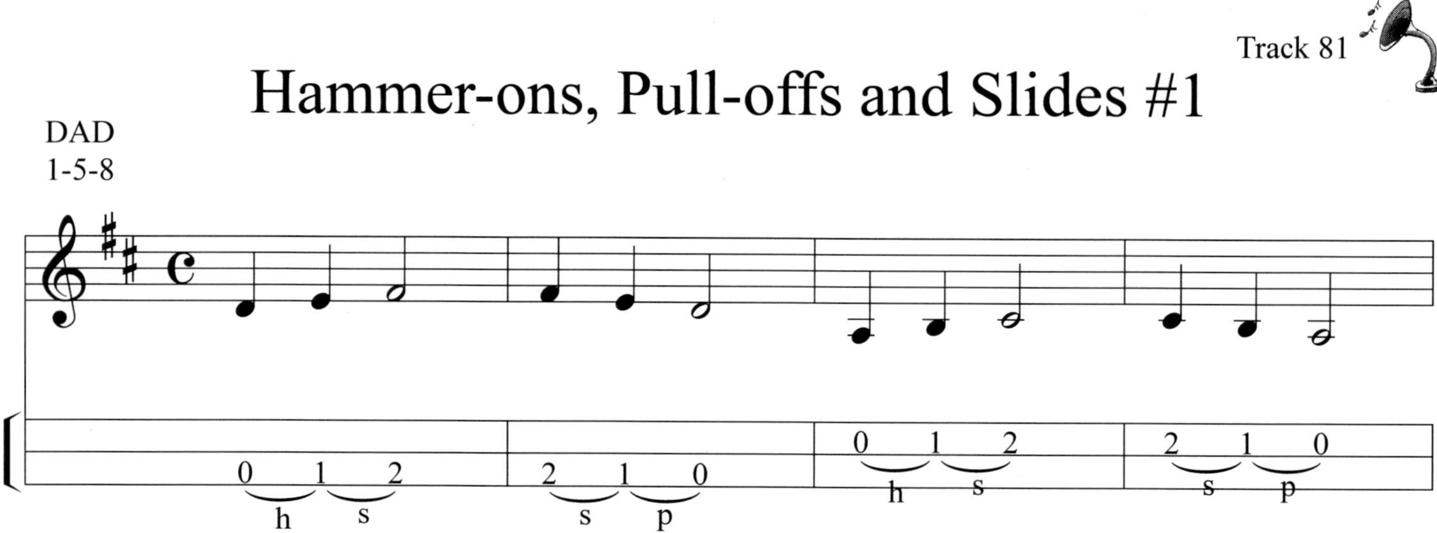

This is a section of a traditional song called, "I Got a Gal at the Head of the Holler." Experiment with using different left hand fingers.

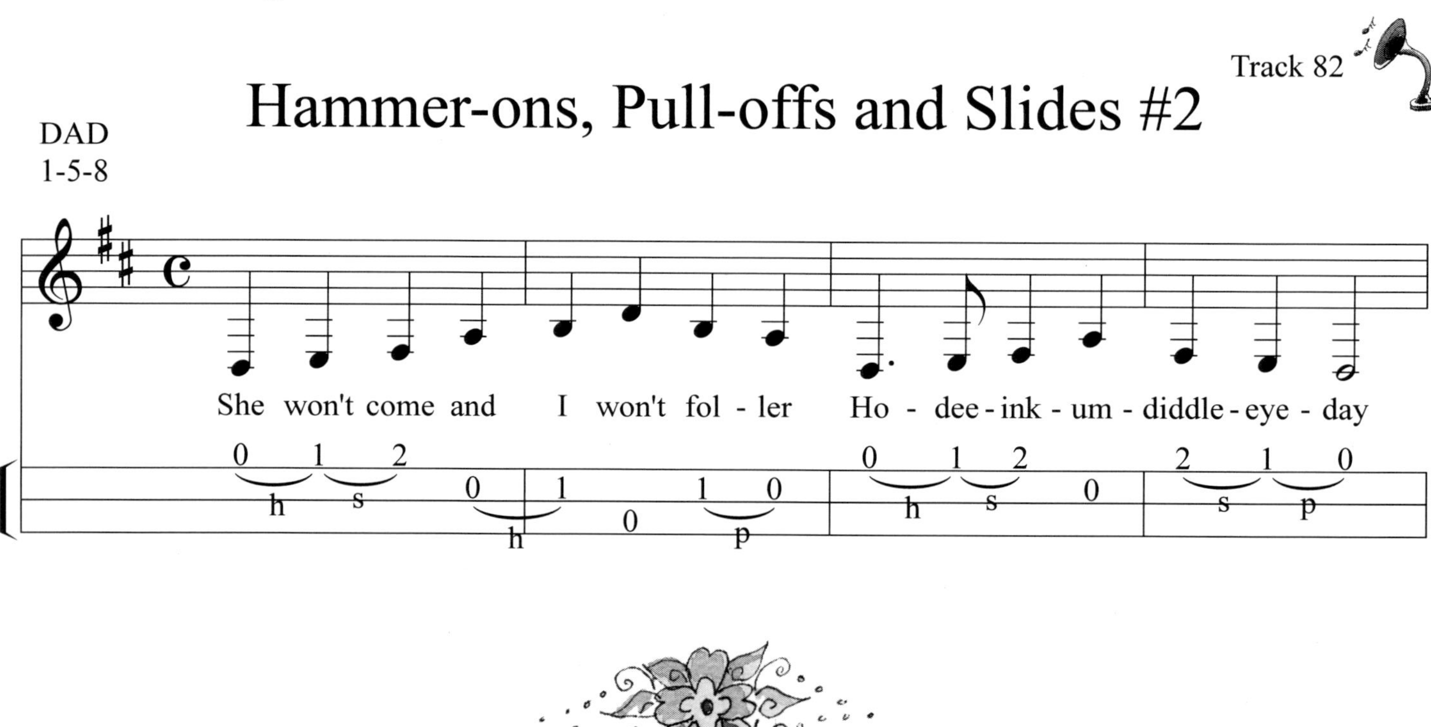

In "Going Home" (a well-known song based on a melody by Dvořák), the first four measures are similar to the last four measures, but I've notated them in very different ways. This should give you an idea of the range of choices that you have when you're making your own decisions as to where to put hammer-ons, pull-offs and slides.

In the third measure you'll find a pull-off from 4i to 2r. Remember to place both fingers on your first string. Then, when you pull off with your index finger, your ring finger will be right there already in place.

Going Home

Hammer-on, pull-off, slide exercise

Antonín Dvořák 1893

"The Trip to Waterville" and "Around the Table" are representative of how you might use these techniques "lightly," just to enhance the flow of the tune.

Track 84

The Trip to Waterville

©2015 Anne Dodson

Here are a couple of tips for "Around the Table":

- Measures #3 and #7 – remember to pick the first note of each measure with your right hand and then let the energy of that "hit" carry you through the rest of the measure.
- Measure #13 – yes, you really do use your thumb for the hammer-on.

Track 85

Around the Table

©2015 Anne Dodson

DAD
1-5-8

For the sops

This would be a good time for you to experiment with hammer-ons, pull-offs and slides on your own. Try putting them into a tune you already know, or just play around on the fretboard and see what you come up with. And remember – if you like something you write, make sure you record it or write it down, or chances are good that it will be gone next time you sit down to play it.

"Leap Frog" came about from experimentation in one of my workshops. Someone asked if you could "hop around" with hammer-ons, pull-offs and slides and this is what happened. I use my middle finger for the whole thing.

Leap Frog

©2015 Anne Dodson

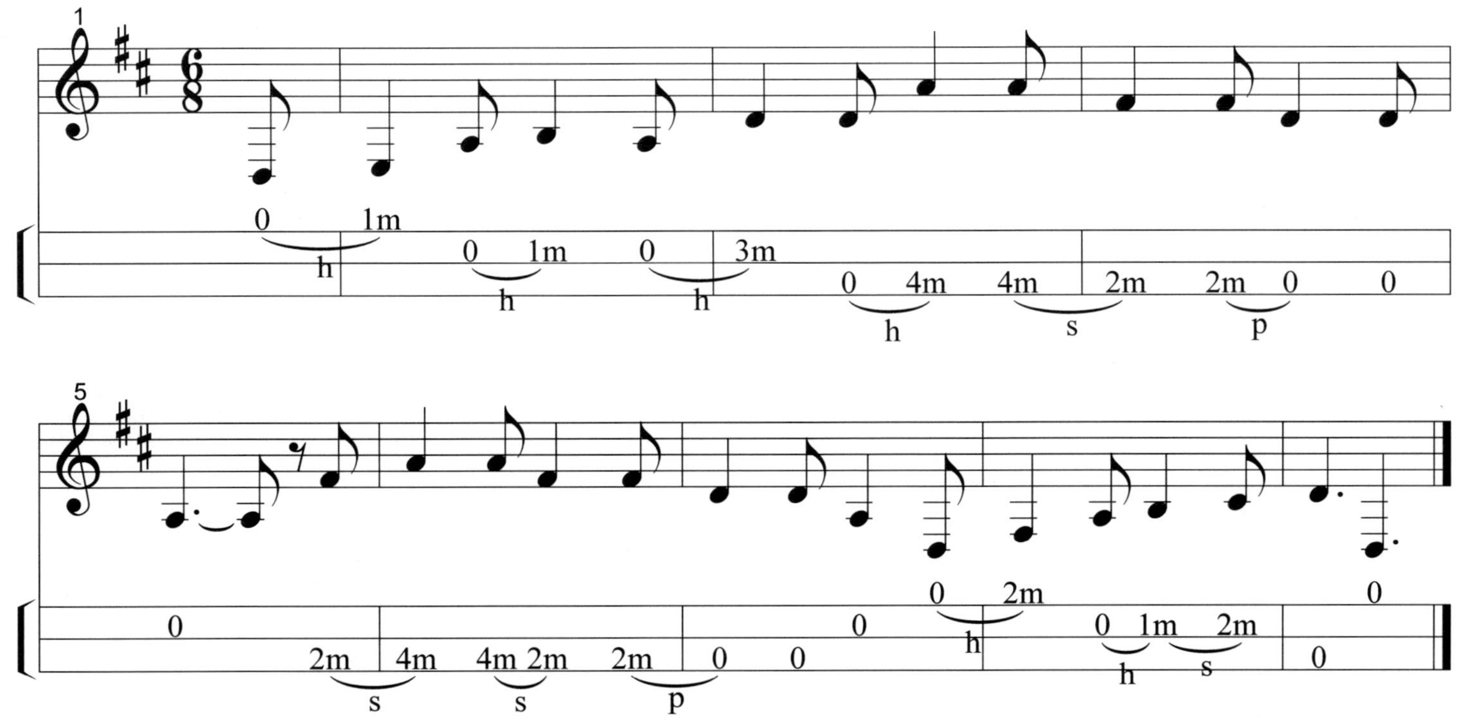

To end this chapter, here's a tune called "Serendipity." It can be played solo, but the two parts can also be played together. It's played mostly on the first string and is meant to be somewhat meditative. Play it with your own internal rhythm – give it lots of space and let those fermatas[1] ring out. Don't let the TAB intimidate you. Its bark is worse than its bite. Take it one step at a time – you can do it.

Tips for learning "Serendipity":
- Isolate measures #2 and #11 and play them a bunch of times before you tackle the whole piece.
- Once you get a feel for how those two measures work, try playing them with the measures that come before and after.
- Now play the whole tune.

---

[1] A fermata is the little "eyebrow" over or under a note. It looks like this: ⌒ . It indicates that you are to pause at your discretion.

Serendipity

©2015 Anne Dodson

DAD
1-5-8

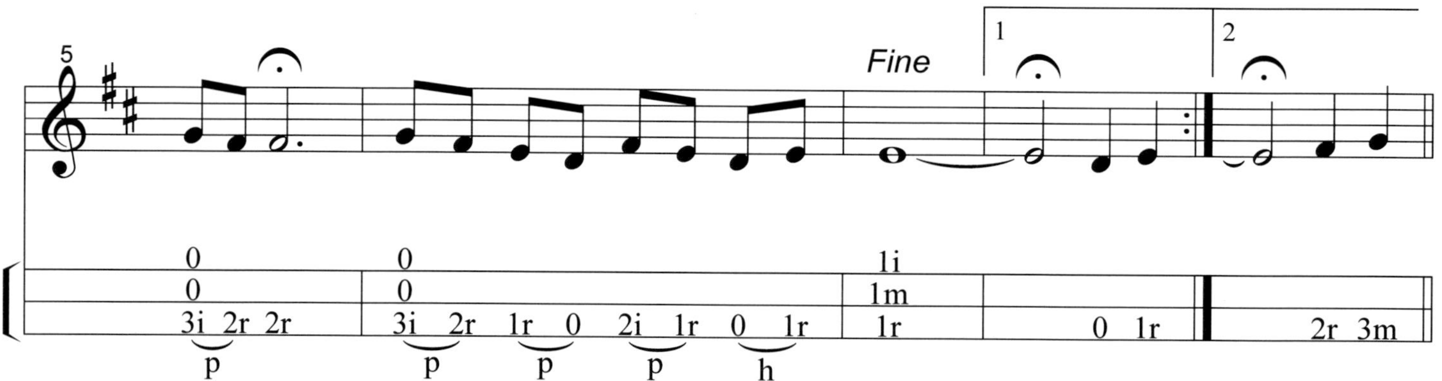

Part B can be played as a harmony to part A

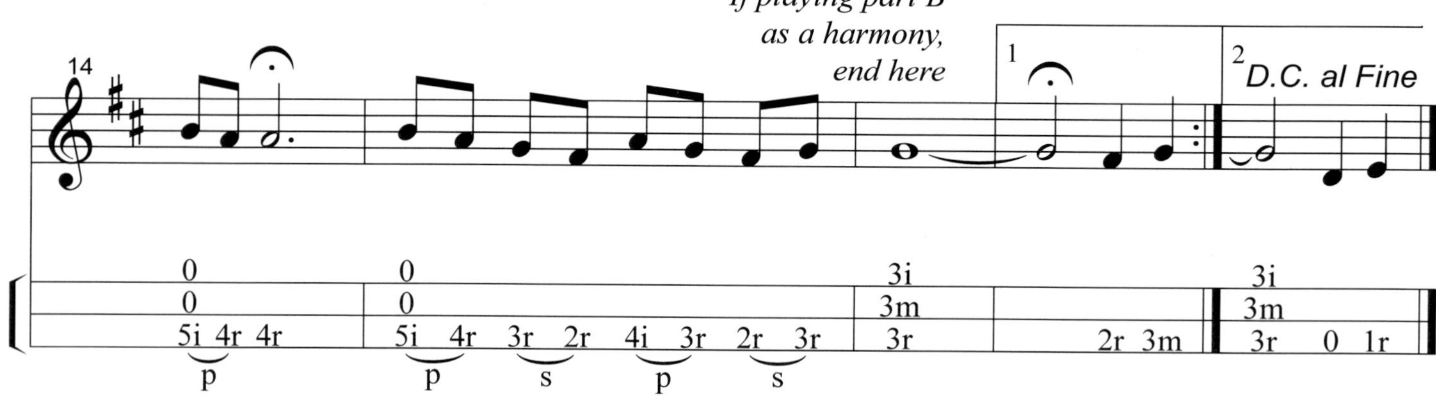

Feel free to try hammer-ons, pull-offs and slides in places where I haven't notated them. Remember, when you're first learning a new piece, it's sometimes easier to leave them out until you get comfortable with the timing and fingering, adding them in when you feel you've got the piece under control.

These three left hand techniques can go a long way toward making your playing more fluid and, let's face it, they really are just downright fun! If you don't believe me yet, give it a little more time – they'll sneak up on you.

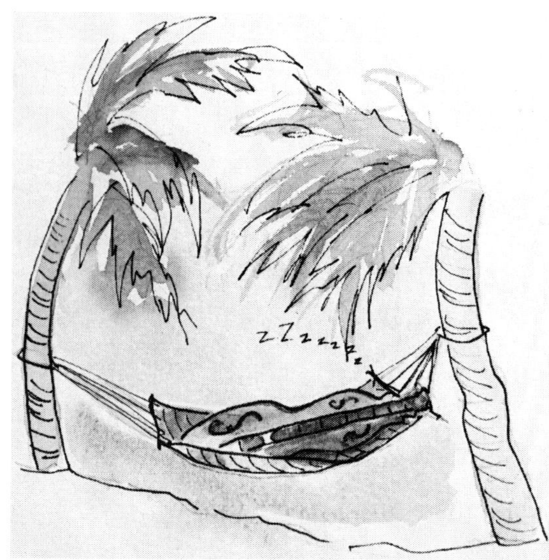

Chapter 8
Take a Break – Level I

Some tunes for you to play

Now it's time for you to take a break from learning new skills and just play a few tunes, but first I hope you'll sit back and appreciate what you've done so far. Flip back through the pages you've worked on and give yourself a pat on the back for hanging in there through some pretty esoteric concepts. Review anything that you weren't too sure about the first time through; I suspect some things might make more sense now, in retrospect.

Before you start in on these tunes, here are a few things to remember about your body:
- Make sure your shoulders stay even and that you're not twisting your body or arms to accommodate your playing.
- Keep the fingers of both hands rounded and relaxed.
- Keep your instrument away from your body, out toward your knees.
- Keep your knees apart to provide a wide base for the instrument.
- Angle the left side of your dulcimer (where the tuning pegs are) out a little farther than the right side.
- Consider using a back-strap (you'll love it, I promise).

And some more things to remember about playing:
- Use consecutive left-hand fingering. No bouncing around with only one finger, please.
- Clap or count out rhythms before playing a piece.
- When possible, keep your left hand finger(s) just behind the indicated fret to get the clearest tone and to eliminate string buzzes. You also don't have to press down as hard if you play there (as opposed to in the middle or – perish the thought – the left of the fret space).
- If you're having problems with a section, isolate the area and work with it until it's no longer a "red flag" that trips you up each time.
- If you feel as if you're juggling too many things at once, eliminate something, i.e., if the left hand is challenging, you can simplify your right hand by strumming instead of fingerpicking.
- Speaking of fingerpicking, if you're a three-string player, use your right thumb for the first string, your index finger on your middle string and either your index or middle finger on the bass string. *The same for you four-string equidistant players, except you can sneak in a pick here and there on your "floating" second string.*
- Unless I've put "direction of strum" arrows in the TAB, use your own discretion as to whether you strum or you pluck.
- Try to recognize specific chords when you see them within the TAB. Give them a name if you can, i.e., if you see "0,1,3" written into the TAB, think to yourself, "ah – there's that first position G chord."
- Use hammer-ons, pull-offs and slides if you find places where they seem natural to *you*, even if they're not marked as such.
- And most of all, give my suggestions a fighting chance, but always overrule me in favor of methods that work for your body and brain processes.
- And, of course, have fun and remember that you're in charge.[1]

That's a long list. You should *really* be impressed with yourself – you've learned a lot!

---

[1] Speaking of "new age" comments, there's an aisle at our local supermarket that says, "wine, crackers and new age." So far I've only found the wine and crackers.

The Tunes

Jingle Bells (page 112):
We start out with a familiar tune, just to give you a leg up. By the way, 0,2,2 is a dissonant chord, but once you're playing up to speed, you'll love it! I include chord suggestions so that you can play with another instrument, or sing the melody and use the chords to accompany yourself singing. If you find that you don't like the F#m and the Bm, you could simplify the accompaniment chords by staying on a D chord through measures #1, #2, #9 and #10. Your call.

All Through The Night (page 113):
Here's another tune I suspect you'll know, using some alternate versions of first position chords. Feeling ambitious? Substitute some second position chords for the first position suggestions I've made.

Sailing Home (page 114):
"Sailing Home" is a slow, contemplative piece. Make sure you give those long, held out notes their full due. *Four-string equidistant players: your open second string may sound wrong to you at measures #7 and #14 (1,2,1). In the recording I avoided that dissonance by plucking strings 1, 3 & 4, leaving out the "offending" second string. Try it both strummed and plucked and see what you prefer.* Extra credit: Once you know how the melody goes, instead of playing this as an instrumental, sing the lyrics, accompanying yourself with the suggested chords. Experiment with different chord positions with your left hand and try varying picking, plucking and strumming with your right.

October's End (page 115):
Asha and I wrote "October's End" – you guessed it – in the late fall of 2003. The melody is built right into the structure of the chords, so this is a good place to pay attention to the chords and try and name them as you go. In other words:
- 1,1,3 = Em
- 2,2,4 = F#m
- 3,3,5 = G
- 5,5,7 = Bm

The Orchard (page 116):
Remember all that work you did with hammer-ons, pull-offs and slides? With "The Orchard," you get to strut your stuff… delicately.

Cold Monday (page 117):
With "Cold Monday," I can't resist talking you through one challenge for your left hand. Before you start, play through the next-to-last measure of each section (measures #7 and #15 – yeah, they're the same thing):
- See that 1,0,1 chord? Play it.
- When you put your thumb down for the second note, leave your fingers in that 1,0,1 position, behind your thumb.
- When you're ready to go to the 2,0,3, leave your thumb down, slide your back fingers up to 2,0,2 (still keeping your thumb on the 3rd fret).
- Play 2,0,3.
- Lift your thumb, and your ring finger will be waiting right there on the 2nd fret for the final note of the measure.
- Then you just slide the 2,0,2 up to the final measure (3,0,3). Isn't that *great*! Isn't that *fun*! Shades of things to come in Book 2!

Jingle Bells

DAD
1-5-8

Traditional

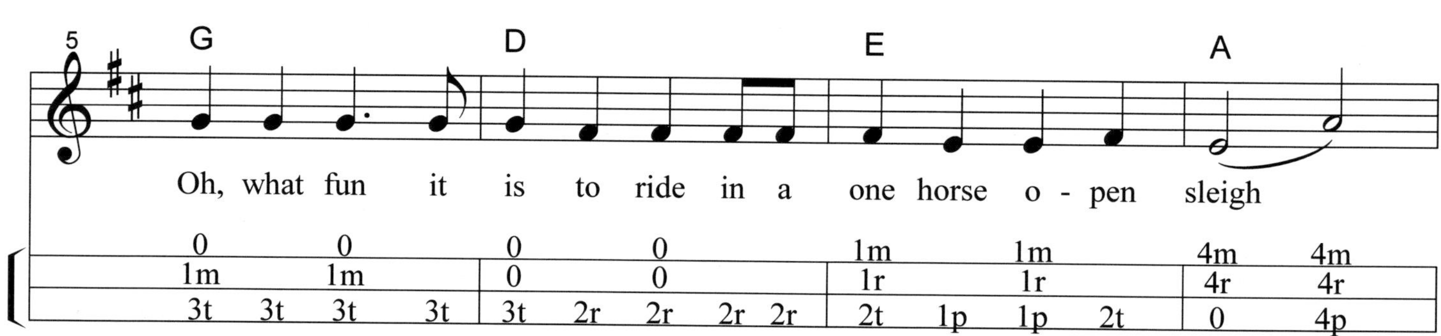

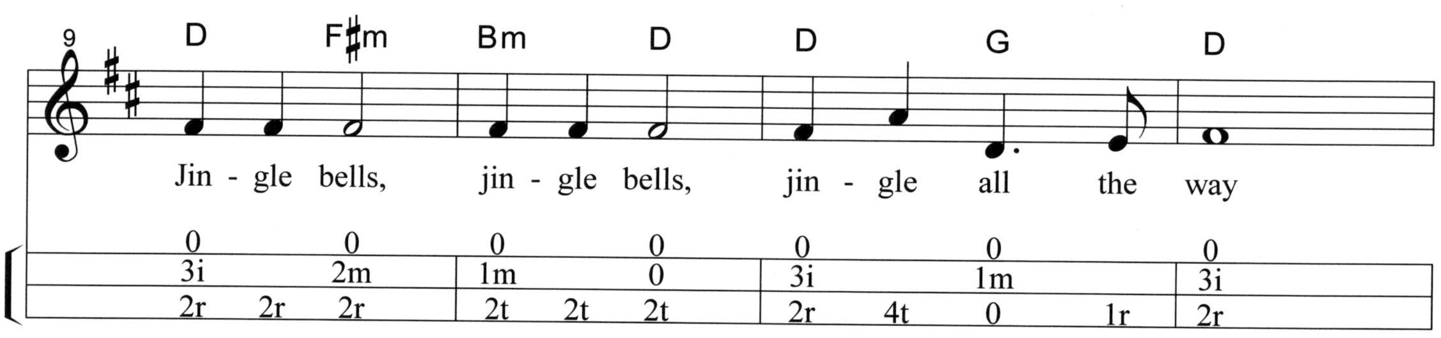

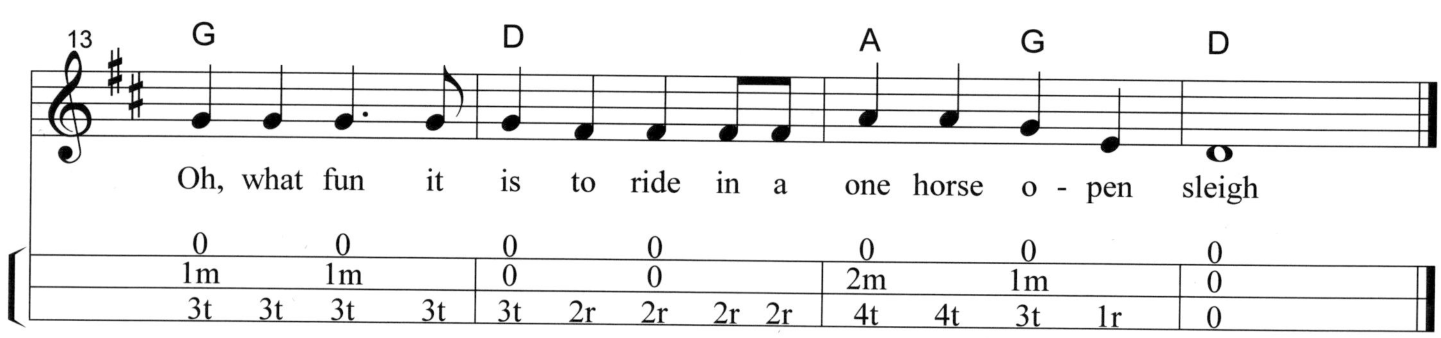

All Through the Night

First position alternate chords

Traditional

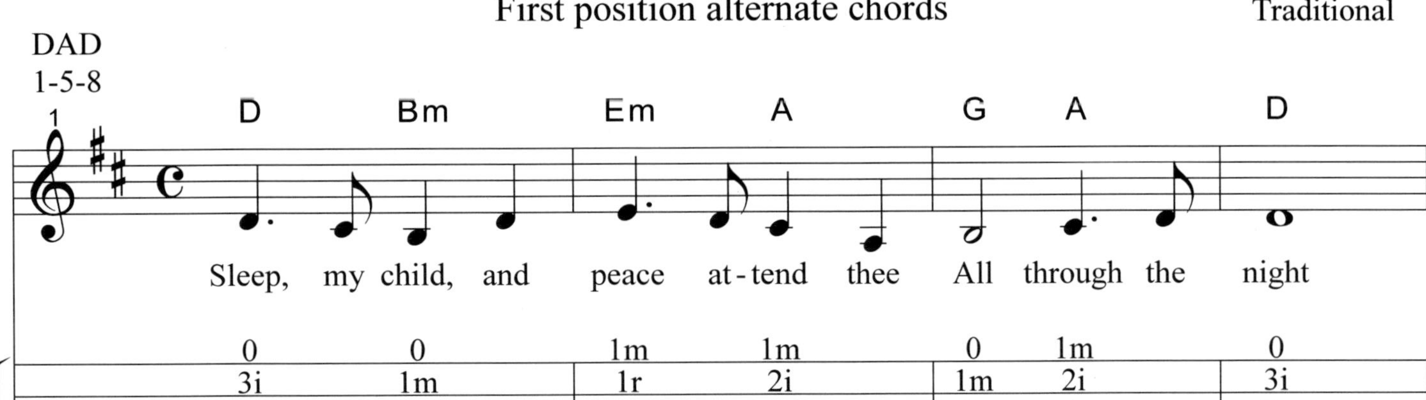

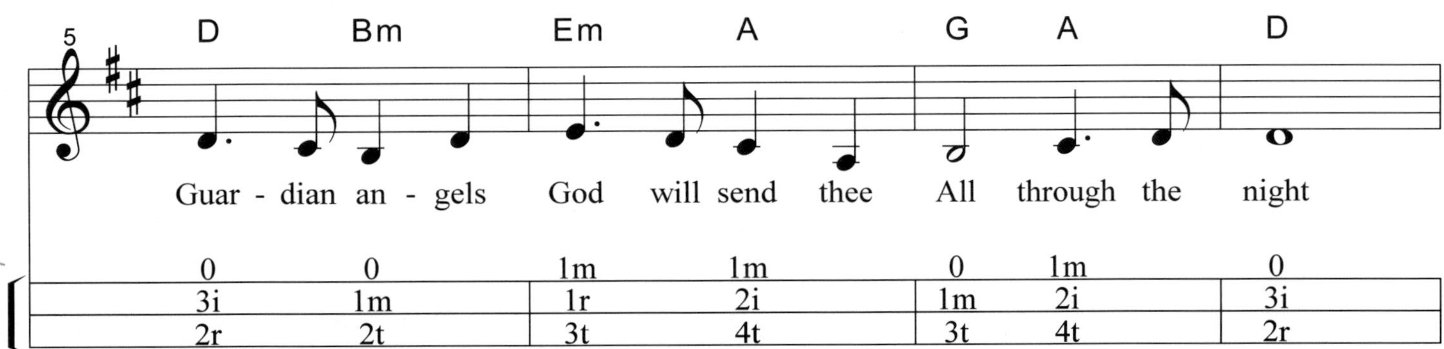

Sailing Home

©2015 Anne Dodson

DAD
1-5-8

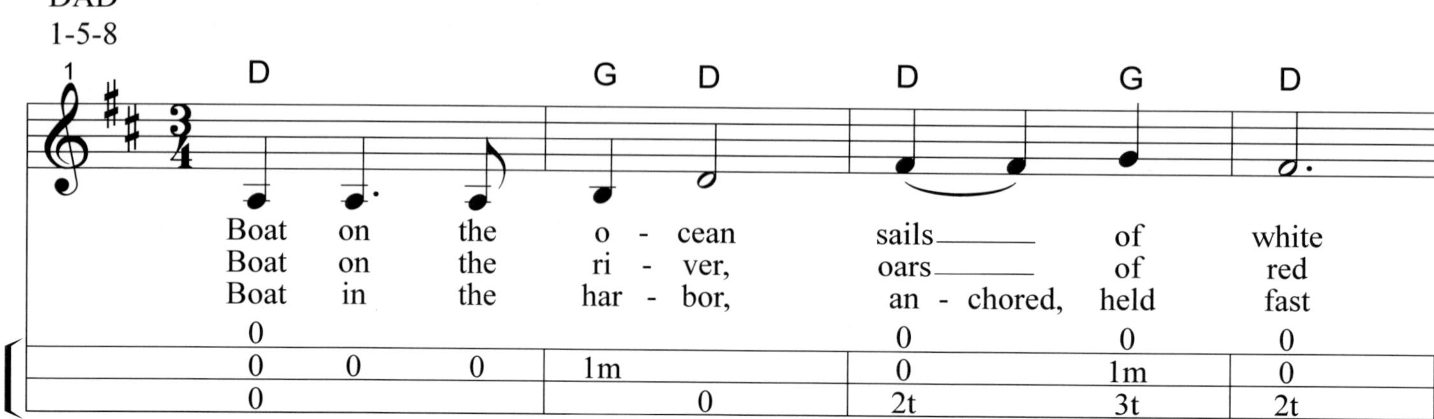

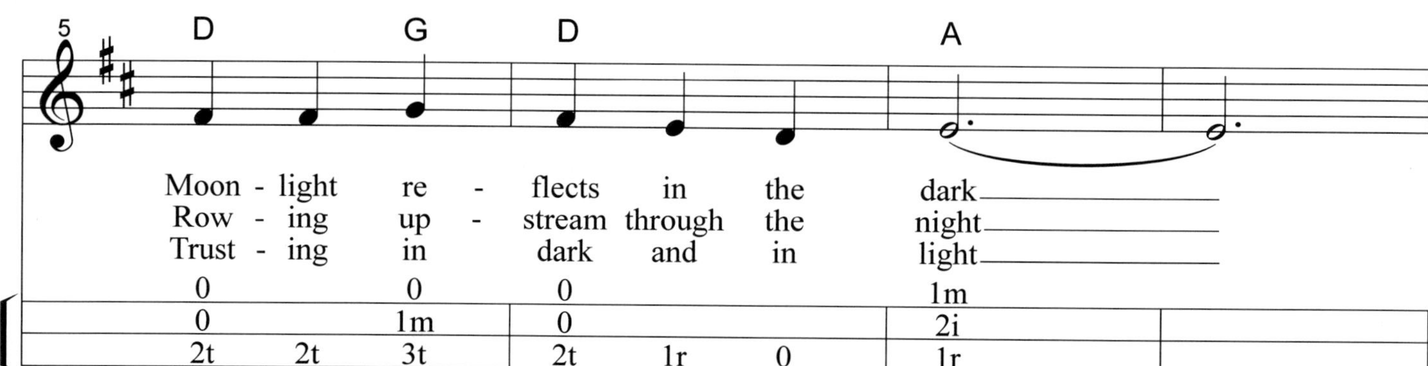

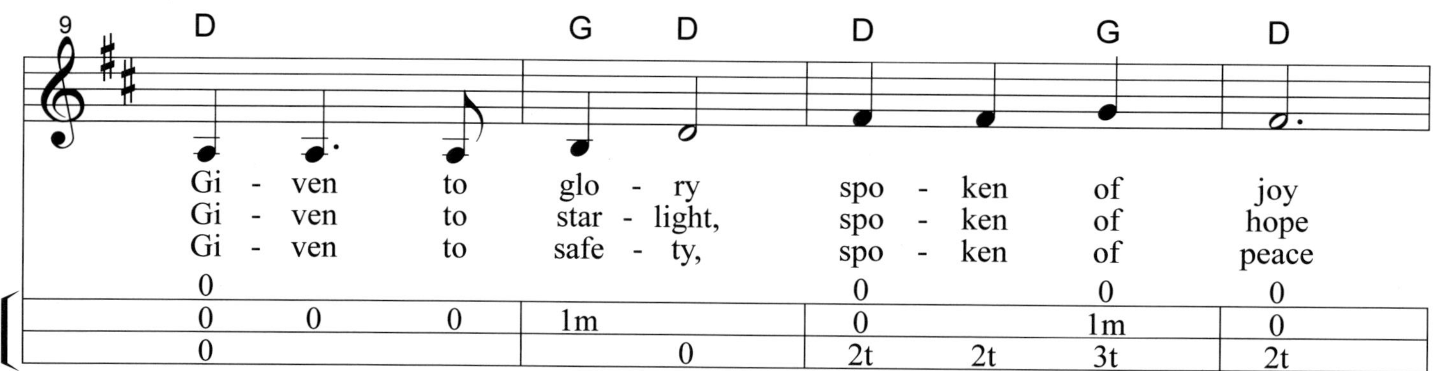

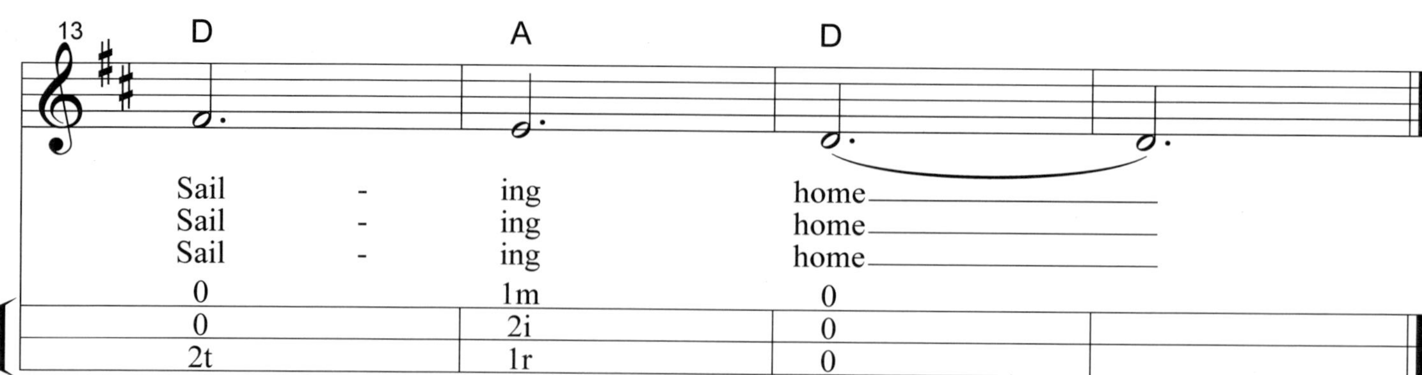

October's End

©2003 Anne E. Dodson & Asha Stager

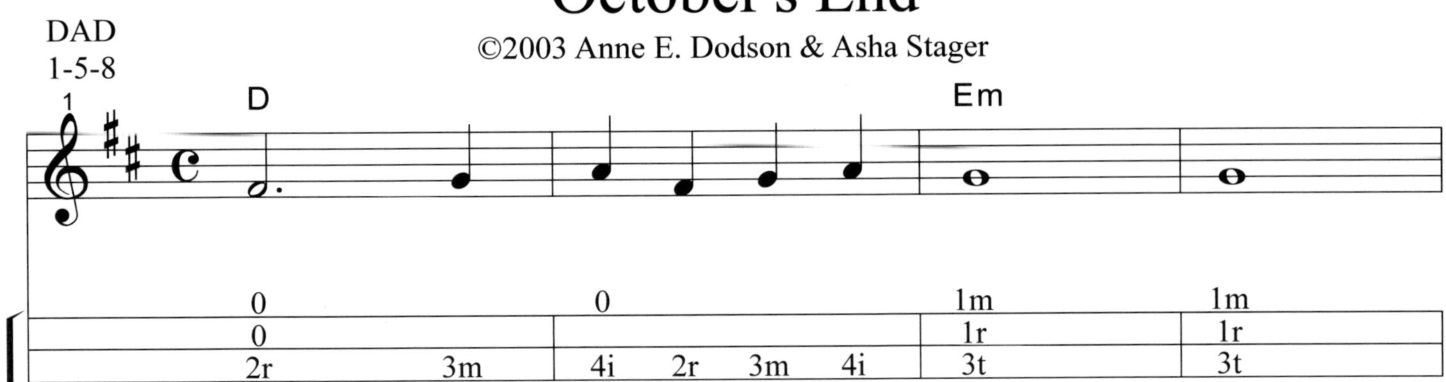

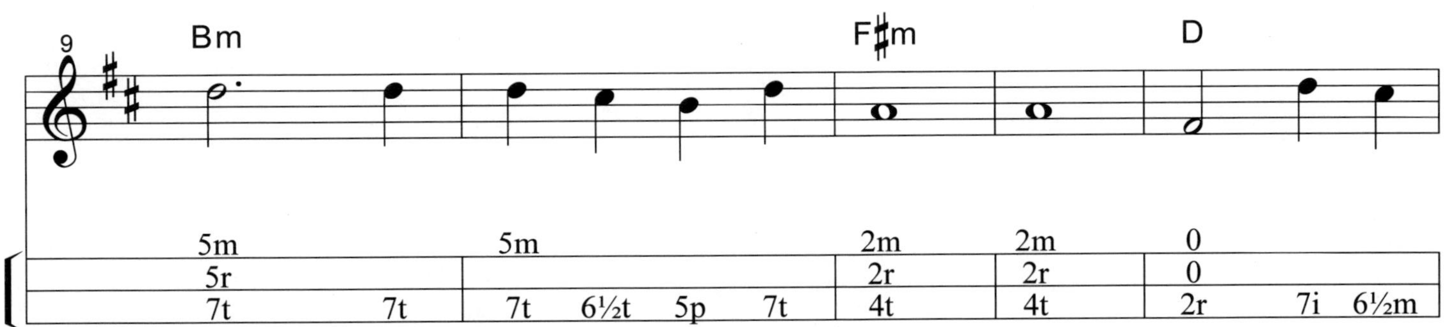

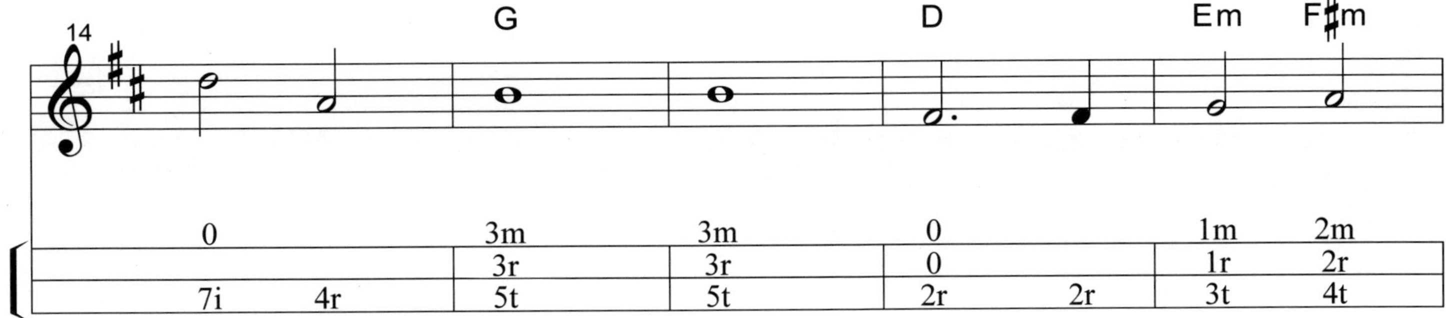

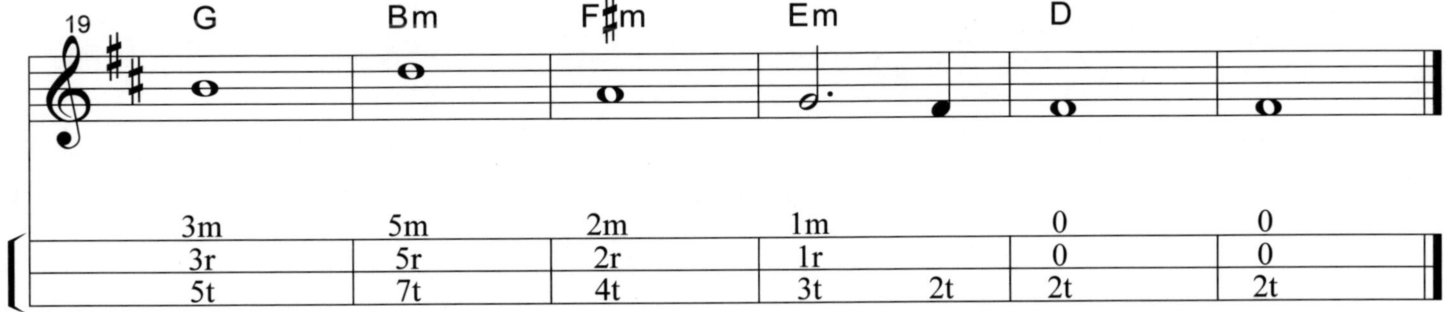

The Orchard

©2015 Anne Dodson

For John & Brien

DAD
1-5-8

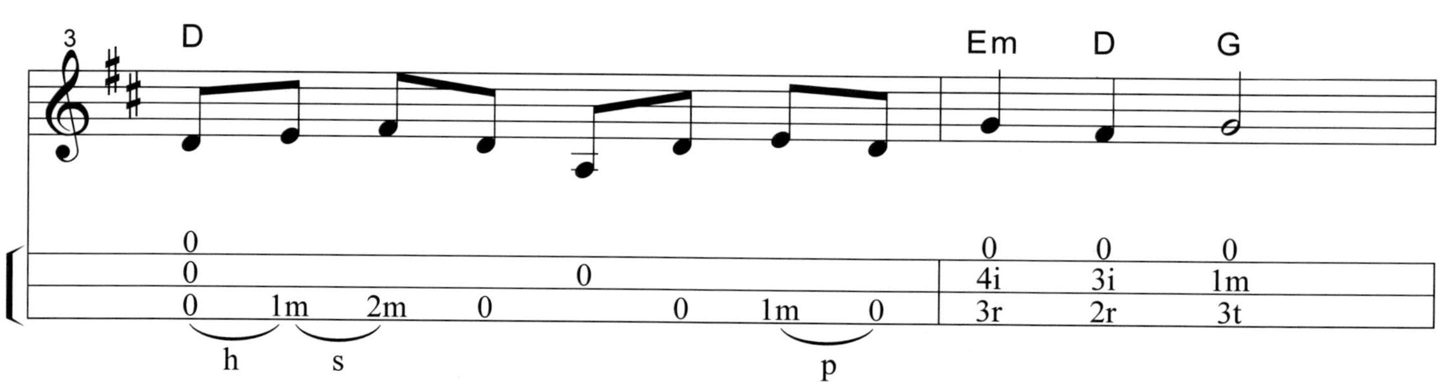

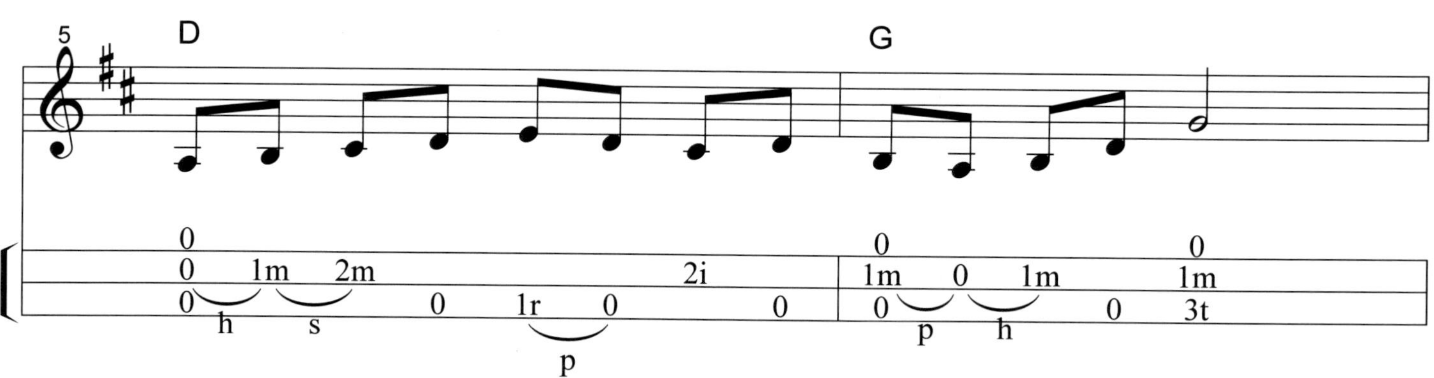

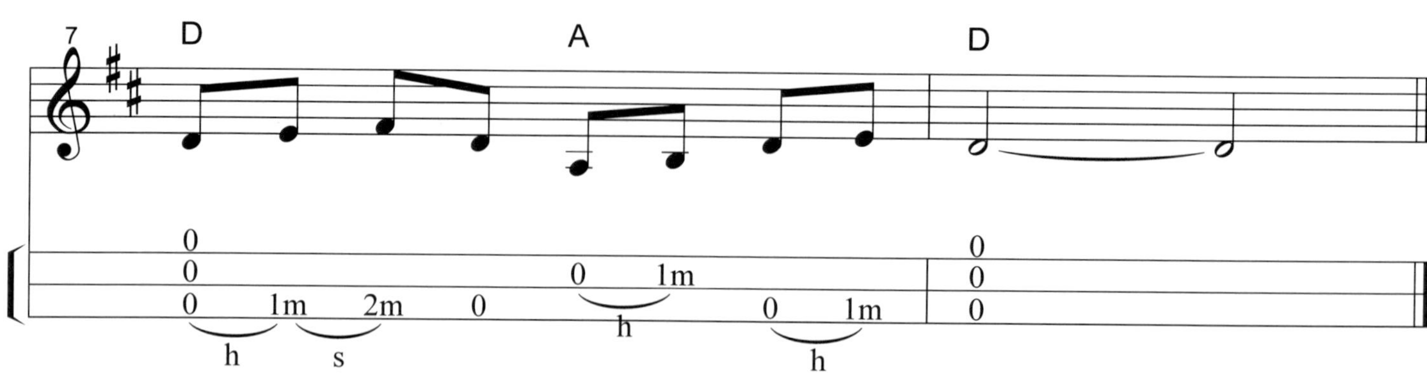

Cold Monday

©2015 Anne Dodson

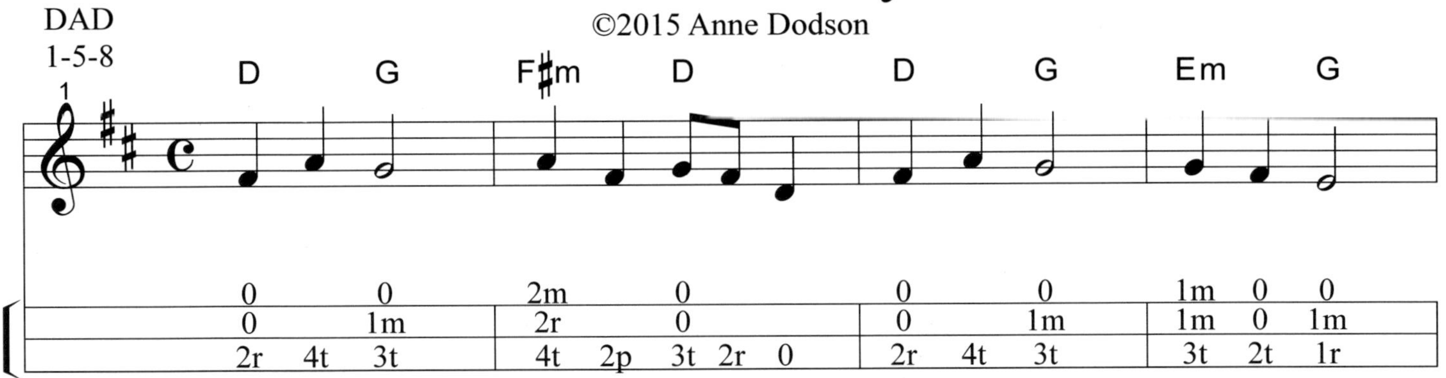

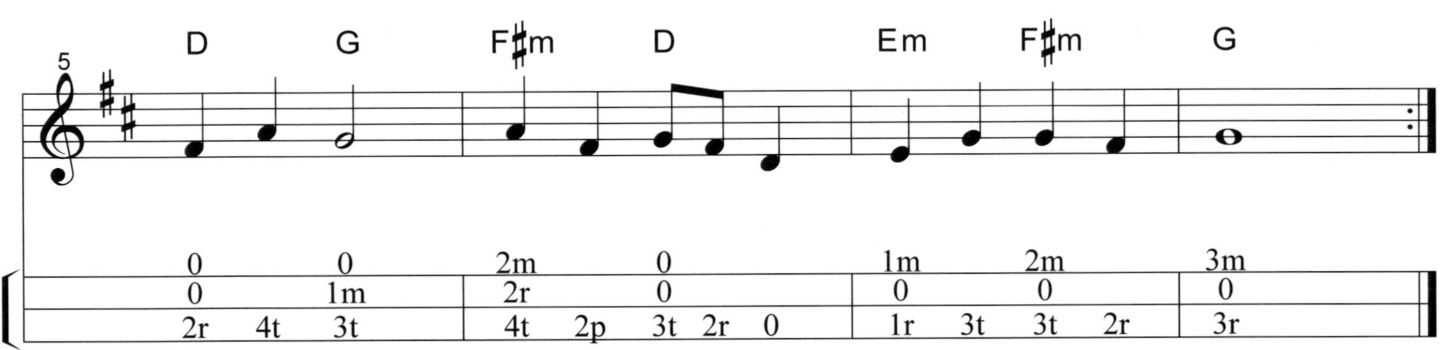

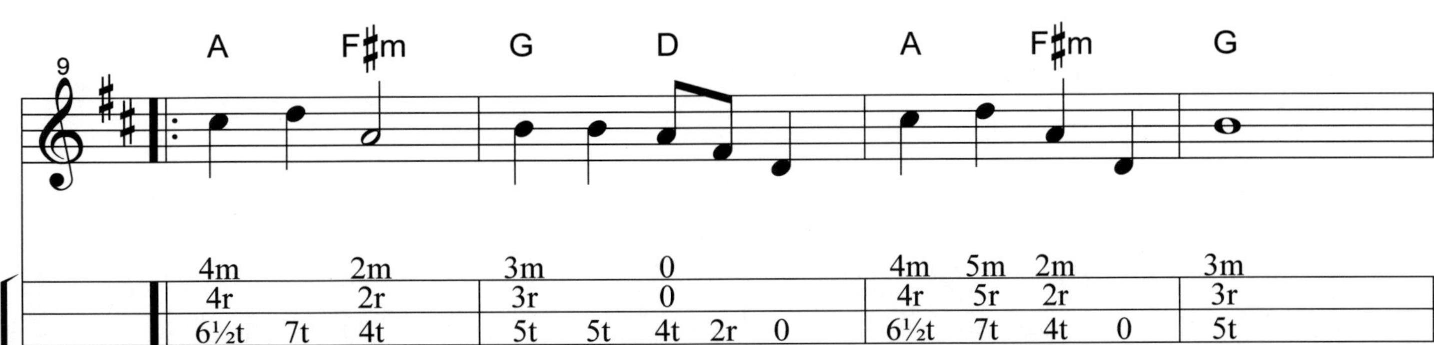

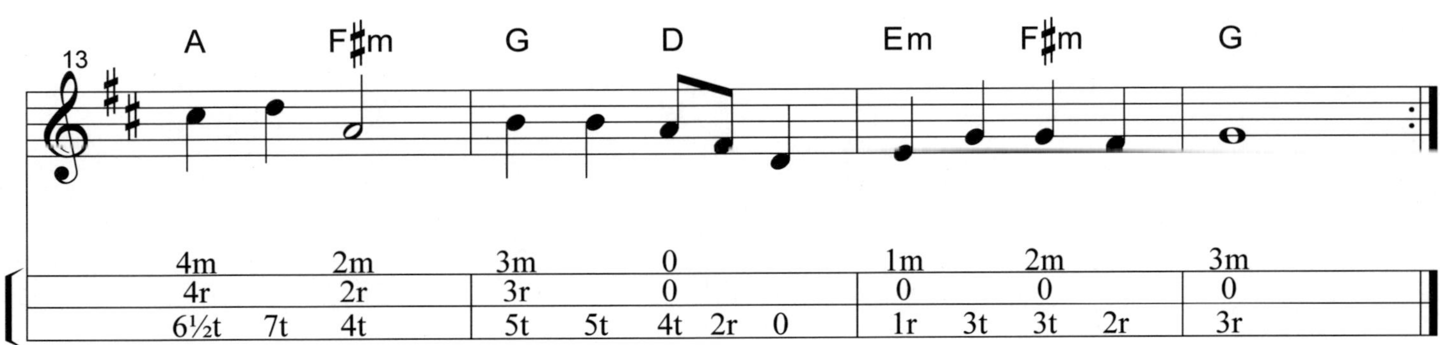

Some final words for Book 1

If there is a tune that you really like, please memorize it. One of the disadvantages of learning from a book is that you can become "paper-trained." Getting off the paper allows you to make the music your own.

I also suggest that you seek out other players from whom you can learn by watching. It can be a challenge, especially if you're used to TAB, but it's so worth the investment.

Find other people to play with. You can make great music with folks who play other instruments, but the sound of two or more dulcimers playing together is pretty darn nice. Playing duets with another dulcimer player (or any instrument for that matter) will force you to play consistently and at an even tempo. And it's fun.

Take a little time and look back through this book. Pick out the tunes that you enjoyed playing and revisit them. You may find that pieces you once thought of as "exercises," or that seemed difficult, have morphed into tunes that are not so hard after all, and that you enjoy playing just for the fun of it!

And then, when you're ready, here's a brief overview of what you can look forward to in Book 2!

An introduction to Book 2 (containing Levels II and III)

Level II branches out into the exploration of other tunings, the use of a capo, how to streamline and add depth and polish to your playing, and suggestions for how to play (nicely) with others. You'll pick up a bit of music theory and learn how it applies to the mountain dulcimer, and you'll find a whole lot more new tunes to play.

Level III builds on what you've learned previously, and encourages you to create your own arrangements by examining chord relationships and experimenting with transposition and scales. There's a special chapter for those of you who play with four equidistant strings, and still more new original tunes.

For further information on Book 2, see Mel Bay Publications, Inc. at www.melbay.com.

Anne Dodson
Camden, Maine

PS:

Have a cup of tea! You've earned it!

Index of Tunes and Songs

About the Author

Anne Dodson was raised in New England and Florida, and grew up in a musical family that would sing at the drop of a hat. She discovered the mountain dulcimer in her late teens while passing through the southern mountains on seasonal commutes between Florida and Maine. Although she plays guitar and penny whistle, the dulcimer has remained her main focus, both as accompaniment for singing and for playing instrumentals.

She has given workshops and performed in concerts and folk festivals around the U.S., Scotland, England and Russia. Although retired from touring, she continues to give private music lessons at her home in Maine. This book is an outgrowth of what she has learned from her students!

Anne has performed throughout her life, beginning in childhood with her brother, David Dodson, and with cousins Tom Heald and Jan (Heald) Appel. Later on, she worked with two groups, "County Down" and "Different Shoes," and most recently has performed solo and with husband, Matt Szostak.

The author begins her career early!

Recordings

County Down: *County Down* (Fretless 1980, currently out of print)
County Down: *Living in the Country* (Fretless 1983, currently out of print)
Different Shoes: *One Size Feets All* (Fretless 1985, currently out of print)
Different Shoes: *Tie One On* (Alcazar 1988, currently out of print)
Anne Dodson: *Tranquility Grange* (Fretless 1986)
Anne Dodson: *In Its Own Sweet Time* (Beech Hill 1990)
Anne Dodson: *From Where I Sit* (Beech Hill 1993)
Anne Dodson: *Almost Grown (for kids and their adults)* (Beech Hill 1995)
Anne Dodson: *Against the Moon* (Beech Hill 2000)

For more information & recordings:
www.annedodson.com